Parenting

backwards

Raising our kids
to become fabulous adults
by looking forward
and working backwards

Bette Levy Alkazian, M.A., LMFT

Parenting Backwards
Second Edition

Copyright © 2013 by Bette Levy
Alkazian

Edited by Karyn Blackmore-Hagy

Illustrations by Cory Issner Jakl
Illustrations Copyright © 2010

Photo on page by Mike Johnsen

Balanced Parenting Publishing
2277 Townsgate Road, Suite 214B
Westlake Village, CA 91361

www.BalancedParenting.com
www.ParentingBackwards.com

Dedicated to

This book is a true collaborative effort of my family, friends, colleagues and clients who I have been blessed to know over the past many years. Thank you for teaching me, encouraging me and inspiring me to share and give back my knowledge and love of parenting in the pages of this book. I have a wonderful family, supportive friends, extraordinary colleagues and faithful clients who continue to teach me every day and to whom I am forever grateful. This book is dedicated to each and every one of you.

With extra special thanks to Karyn Blackmore-Hagy. Karyn, without you, this book never would have gotten past square one. Thank you for helping me to find my voice as a writer and for adding humor to the book and to the process of writing it! You're my hero!

Sometimes an angel appears in your life and you wonder what you did to deserve this. Michelle Gradis, you are an angel on this earth to me. Thank you for your help with this Second Edition.

BLA

Table of Contents

Forward for "Parenting Backward"

I've never met a parent who didn't want what's best for their children. Every day, I see parents with hopes and dreams: that their children will become independent adults who can make a contribution – and even achieve great things. But parents often lack the instruction manual on how to make that happen.

While parenting doesn't come with a road map, "Parenting Backward" provides an excellent starting point. This is especially important today, when the parenting dynamic has changed so much from prior generations.

This book starts with a brilliant conceit: determining where you want your children to be when they are adults, and then working backward to identify the steps needed to get them there. It's a goal-setting solution that will work for the rest of our lives, and it provides a great pathway for raising successful children. Using this concept can help you raise your children to be successful, respectful, independent, and more.

We often hear about a lack of values, goals, and coping skills in today's youth. I see it every day in my practice. Many parents simply don't know how to start teaching these important elements. This book will provide parents with the insight and guidance they need to tackle those areas. From working through those hard-to-love moments to raising independent children and finding your own passion, this book covers all the bases.

Issues such as teen pregnancy, drug use and bullying dominate headlines and community conversations. From the high drop-out rates in schools to the number of adult children who are moving back home to live with their parents, and many issues in between, there is often something missing in today's parenting.

"Parenting Backwards" is a step in the right direction and helps solve these problems. Parents will come away with a clear idea of how to help raise their children to become the adults they envision them to be. The information and advice in this book is useful to all families and can help them get, and keep, their parenting on the right track. Forget just parenting… parent backward!

Tanya Altmann, MD, FAAP
Pediatrician, author and mom

Preface

My mother is a funeral director.

Is that a great way to start a book, or what? Being a therapist, you can't write this one any better! Sometimes truth really is stranger than fiction! Now don't get me wrong, I love my mother and she didn't spend my entire childhood in that occupation, but it has made for some interesting experiences, most of them (luckily) humorous. I think we can all look back at our childhood and remember great things about our parents and well, not so great things. It's normal. But we always have to remember that no parent is perfect.

The main point here is not to blame your parents. They did their best given their own circumstances, mixed in with their own upbringing. You need to move on. In fact, many of us will most likely parent "just like our parents". GASP! For some of you, I know you are smiling at that. You are the lucky few! For others (most of us that is), you need to put this book down and have a good cry and call your brother or your sister. The thought of becoming your parents can make you...well...concerned. It's ok. Just remember to take the bad, vow not to repeat it, and savor the happy memories – the things your parents did well (come on now they did something well) and "parent from the positive". (More on this in Chapter 3.)

Remember, one day your kids will also be judging you as parents when they become parents themselves. It is a generational thing...a fact of life. Every parent thinks they can do things differently and be better than their parents. So do that. Reading this book is a great start. Parents have been around for millions of years...and so have kids. We all have a lot to draw upon.

If you're reading this book, you're more likely to have put on lipstick today (or at least thought you did) instead of a tie. What I mean by that is that you're probably a woman. The reason I bring this up is because you need to rein in your man or your partner in parenting to read this book with you. Parenting is a partnership. You are a team from the start. It takes two to make a baby and a whole village to raise a baby!

Enjoy!

Introduction

*"If I see an ending, I can work **backward**."*
Arthur Miller

*"One of the first things one notices in a **backward** country is that children are still obeying their parents." Anonymous*

What is *Parenting Backwards*?

Let's talk about my eulogy. Here I go again, talking about death and funerals. Hang in there. This will make sense in a minute.

I experienced a motivational tool used by a Life Coach at a workshop once. It was suggested that I should write my own eulogy. Many people in the room squirmed at that thought, but because of my mom being a funeral director, death has never been a taboo subject in my family! Stay with me, here.

The goal was to write my own eulogy and then to work backwards toward living up to those words. Try it...it isn't that easy. Writing a eulogy that might be read (heaven forbid) tomorrow? It was very morbid to think about, but it really made me focus on how my life would be measured by those I love – especially my daughters.

My eulogy was long and filled with things I clearly wanted to do better. Two traits that stuck out to me in my eulogy were that I was a compassionate person and a great parent. Now the hard part…how was I going to live up to those words especially for my daughters? If I was going to be at my own funeral, looking down and listening and not being able to argue one word, what would I want my daughters to remember and to say? My husband? My friends? Whew…it's a lot to think about but it is a great exercise and a terrific first step. Change can be a wonderful thing.

Writing my eulogy made me think about a poem written by Michael Josephson entitled *What Will Matter*. It talks about all the things that really *DON'T matter* when faced with death and the world after you've gone…and the things that really *DO matter* and the choices you have to make to create a life that truly matters. It is all so relevant to being a good parent and the daily example we set for our kids by showing them what

really *MATTERS* to us! Here is an excerpt:

What will matter is not what you bought, but what you built;

not what you got, but what you gave.

What will matter is not your success, but your

significance.

What will matter is not what you learned, but what

you taught.

What will matter is every act of integrity, compassion,

courage and sacrifice that enriched, empowered or

encouraged others to emulate your example.

What will matter is not your competence, but your

character.

What will matter is not how many people knew you,

but how many will feel a lasting loss when you're

gone.

What will matter is not your memories, but the

memories of those who loved you.

What will matter is how long you will be remembered,

by whom and for what.

Living a life that matters doesn't happen by accident.

It's not a matter of circumstance but of choice.

Choose to live a life that matters.

Parenting Backwards is based on a similar "eulogy" exercise to the one I did in the workshop. However, this time, the question is:

"Who do you want your kids to be when they're grown up?"

For example, if I want my daughters to be responsible, then what do I have to do while they're young to ensure that they learn responsibility? If I want them to be kind and compassionate, what do I have to do today to teach them what kindness and compassion are and why I think they are important?

Parenting Backwards is about creating a vision and then making it happen step by step, day by day.

THE PARENT DISCLAIMER:

Of course, there are no guarantees that our kids will grow up to become who we envision or imagine they should become. They are individuals and will become who they want to be. My goal is that we, as parents, be intentional about what we are modeling and teaching to our kids. At the end of our parenting job, I want every parent to be able to say, "I did the best job I knew how to do! I thought about it and I modeled making a good life for my kids." The rest is truly up to them.

When I was growing up, Dr. Spock wrote the only parenting book on my parents' shelf. I'm not actually sure if my parents even read it. There wasn't a lot of thought put into parenting in those days. Parents did what they thought was best and basically "shot from the hip". There was little intention in their parenting. Even so, they did a pretty good job.

There has been so much research done in the past 40 years on parenting and many books have been written. In addition, we are raising kids in a different world than the one in which I was raised. There is little tolerance for spanking, yelling and harsh punishment in today's world. In fact, kids are the first ones to tell their parents, "I'll call Child Protective Services on you!" We live by different standards, to say the least. However, the saying, "the more things change, the more they stay the same," is also true. The basic role of a parent has not changed.

Our legal obligation is to provide a roof over their heads, clothes on their backs and food on the table. For all of us over-achievers, we also expect ourselves to provide love, discipline, respect, compassion, etc...

The respect system in families is also upside-down from when I grew up. We have to earn our kids' respect now, not bully them into submission or parent with a fear-based discipline system. It's actually a better system. If you want to raise your kids to be respectful, then raising them in a respect-based home is the best way to do so. Listen first, then react. If you want to be listened to, you need to listen. It's amazing what we can learn if we adopt a more "innocent until proven guilty approach".

In the *Parenting Backwards* Philosophy, we have our eye on the target at all times.

Who do you hope your child becomes? What traits do you hope your child will possess?

Respectful
Responsible
Capable
Caring
Compassionate
Resilient
Independent
Thoughtful
Etc…

So, how do we get from here to there? This book is meant to be a road map, of sorts. To help you think about your parenting and to be intentional about it. I hope to introduce thoughts you might not have considered before, to give you tools and even the words to carry out some of your goals.

The age range targeted in this book is broad and covers all of the years of parenting, though I didn't address parenting teens, specifically, in most cases. Many of the parenting tools you use at a young age can definitely be applied to later years. For example, a 16 year old is just as capable and likely of a temper tantrum as a 4 year old. Trust me, I know!

In writing this book, I have thought a lot about who I am in this process and my relationship with my readers. I want to convey a feeling of camaraderie. I'm in the trenches with you raising my kids, too. Do I want to be the go-to parenting expert? Yes, I do, but not from a throne or a pedestal. I want to be sitting right there next to you saying, "This is hard, isn't it? But we're in it together!"

I have this fear that I will leave my sliding glass door open on a beautiful spring day and someone will hear me yelling at my kids or having a meltdown moment of some sort. I can just see it now, plastered on the cover of the morning newspaper:

I have my moments, just like any other parent. I do my best and work hard to keep my parenting tool belt on and reach for the right tools at the right times, but I'm not perfect. In fact, I don't even aspire to be perfect. I invite you to aspire to be better and to do as great a job as you can with your kids, but please don't be perfect! Your kids just want you to be you. In fact, I lost my temper last night with my daughter, Mollie. She even called me on it, showing me that I was being totally unreasonable. GUILTY! Then, I said, "You know what? You're right. I'm actually mad at your dad and I'm taking it out on you. I'm so sorry." I think that the value in losing my temper and then having an honest dialogue about it was probably more valuable than had I held it together from the beginning. (Not that I recommend losing our temper any more than is absolutely necessary. Just be honest about it when you do!) Let your kids see that you make mistakes and that you are capable of owning up to them.

I was very blessed in my life to have an amazing supervisor, therapist and mentor. Her name was Eileen Fond. I loved her, admired her and aspired to be just like her. In truth, I really liked who I was through her eyes. She saw something in me that I didn't yet see and through her eyes, I was able to see the good in myself. Not to mention the fact that she helped my husband and me put our marriage back together (more than once) when we had gotten off track. I will forever be grateful to her.

Sadly, Eileen died several years ago, but I still carry her on my shoulder. Often, I say to myself, "What would Eileen say?" when I'm at a loss for words or I'm looking to tap into my best and most wise self.

Do you have an "Eileen"? Do you have someone that you can talk to in times of trouble? Do you have a little angel on your shoulder that can help you see all sides and perspectives?

It is my humble hope to inspire you. After reading this book, perhaps you'll ask yourself, "What would Bette say?" when you're not sure how to handle a situation with your kids. I was floored one morning when one mom appeared at a "Coffee with Bette" gathering wearing a shirt saying "What Would Bette Say?" It made me feel good that I was that little angel on her shoulder. It was a little embarrassing and incredibly flattering. "Coffee with Bette" is a monthly, informal gathering where moms with kids of all ages can bring their questions to me in a very relaxed environment over coffee.

I want my clients and students to ask themselves, "What would Bette say", not because I have all of the answers, but because I hope that it inspires them to tap into that part of themselves that already knows the answers, the way Eileen inspires me every day to do the same.

I'm writing this book because I have a passion for good parenting, not all of the answers. Perhaps I have some good training and experience, but most of all I have a desire to travel this road with you and to make this journey fun. Really, it can be fun! It's a parenting adventure.

Chapter One

Bring on the Fun!!!

"Fun is about as good a habit as there is!"
Anonymous

All of this talk about doing a good job
with our parenting can make it seem like
an ominous task. Let's stay focused on
remembering to have a good time
throughout the process and not let the
enormity of the responsibility weigh us
down.

I feel very lucky that my life is filled with
a lot of laughter. Life can be pretty
heavy at times, but if we can laugh in
the face of fear, we can overpower it. If
we can laugh through our anger, we can
neutralize it. If we can laugh at a funeral
remembering the good times, we can
believe that we can get through it. It
also reminds us of the balance of life.
Even in our darkest moments, there is a
spark of light. Laughter is a great tool to
teach our kids. We all need to learn to
tap into life's lighter moments and have
the perspective to know the difference.

Raising kids, though it feels like it will last forever, is really a short time in the scheme of your whole life. If you spend all of that time worrying, saying "no", correcting, cleaning, and putting toys away, you'll miss this minute. In this minute is an opportunity to enjoy your kids. To have a laugh or share a story. To watch a funny movie or go for a funny walk. Look at old family photos – those are always good for a laugh!

My kids are growing up so quickly. I still see myself as the mother of young kids, yet I have one already in college! How did that happen? Where did the time go? It's almost like a cruel joke. Just when I've gotten attached to these cute, little, adorable beings, and then **BOOM** they're getting bigger and more independent of me every day. They really aren't ours to keep, our kids are just for us to borrow for a short time and then we have to let them go and let go of any sense of ownership.

Oh, wait! This was supposed to be about fun and I'm now completely depressed! Once again, we're talking about balance. The joy of raising kids is constantly balanced by the grief that comes with every developmental leap as they grow away from us. You'll sob at preschool graduation and then, SNAP! before you know it, you'll be pulling out the tissues at their high school graduation.

How are we supposed to get completely attached to these little babies and then work every day from then on to teach them to separate from us? How are we supposed to make sense of this on a daily basis?

What I'm actually asking of you in this book is to remain cognizant of this fact, if only in the back of your minds. To remain aware of the end goal even while feeling stuck in the quagmire of the developmental stage your child is in, which may feel as though it will last forever!

Back to the fun stuff...

Ok, back to having fun! What is the most fun you can have? Laughing, right? A good, hearty belly-laugh is not only great fun; it's also proven to have positive physiological effects. The oxygen our bodies and brains get, the endorphins that get released in our brains! It's almost as good as an hour-long workout at the gym! Ok, I made that up, but it feels great, right?

Some days we just don't feel like laughing. Well, those are the days when we need to laugh the most. Just when things are feeling out of control, that's when we need a good laugh most of all. We need to bring in some humor to lighten up the mood, and we need some laughter to bring a new, fresh perspective on the situation.

How do I laugh when I'm not feeling it? You could actually just start laughing artificially and your body will still respond as if you were seeing the funniest thing ever! Ok, that might feel weird. How about watching an old sitcom on TV? You could watch an old slapstick comedy movie that you haven't seen since you were a kid! I always belly-laugh at the TV show, America's Funniest Videos. There's nothing funnier than watching people do stupid things that make them fall down, right?!

In fact, laughing with your family, your spouse, your kids, or anyone is a great relationship builder and everyone comes away with a great feeling that a good time was had by all! It's all about the relationships and how you show up in them!

Choosing Your Perspective

The beauty of this life is that in every moment we have choices. Lots of choices. We aren't always aware of them, but they are still there. I love this awareness and believe it is essential that we teach it to our kids, as well.

If you are grumpy, you are making that choice. If you are angry, you are making THAT choice. If you are happy, you are also making that choice. Even when things aren't going our way, we can make a different choice than to be unhappy about it. It's learning to understand that we can't control everything. It's also learning that life is easy when all is going well. Our true test of character is challenged when things don't go our way. That is when we grow the most.

I'm not saying we should all be happy all of the time. That's not realistic, nor would it teach our kids what we want them to know about coping with all that life has to offer. However, there are times when we are choosing to be cranky, angry, depressed, grumpy, etc... when it's not necessary and not healthy for our family relationships and especially for our kids.

Life is filled with stresses. Our task is to learn to balance them and even conquer them. We have so many tools at our disposal, that we have no good excuses not to employ all of the tools at our disposal for the sake of spending healthy, quality time with our family.

So, no more using stress as an excuse not to have a good relationship with your spouse! No more using stress as an excuse not to play with your kids. The measure of the person is how he or she handles things in the tough times. Be a good role model and add some much-needed laughter into your family!

"Never take life seriously. Nobody gets out alive anyway." Anonymous

Chapter Two

Clarifying Our Values:
Mt. Olympus vs. Mt. Vesuvius

Ok, back to *Parenting Backwards*.

Mt. Vesuvius, in Italy, is believed to be one of the most dangerous and most active volcanoes in the history of the world. It destroyed the City of Pompeii, among others, and is responsible for tens of thousands of deaths during its many violent eruptions.

Mt. Olympus, on the other hand, the highest mountain in Greece, was believed to be the home of the beautiful, golden palaces of 12 Greek Gods, and it also housed the throne of Zeus, the supreme ruler of the Olympians.

Given the choice, which one would you want to visit? Violent volcano or beautiful palaces?

I use these two mountains as metaphors when working with parents as an illustration of whether they are headed toward chaos or order. It's a dramatic illustration, but an effective one.

How do we know in which direction we're headed...Mt. Vesuvius or Mt. Olympus?

Any successful business has a mission statement. A company's mission statement states the beliefs, aims, objectives, priorities, and goals in working together. It gives direction and states the purpose of the organization. Wouldn't it be great if your family had a mission statement? Then, periodically, you could review it and know if you are headed toward Mt. Olympus or Mt. Vesuvius.

- What is your family's mission statement?
- What is your family's purpose?
- What are your beliefs/values?
- What are your goals as a group?
- What direction do you want your family headed toward?

Note: Develop a Family Mission Statement (FMS) together. This is a great exercise for your kids and lets you know where their priorities are or are not.

Teaching our kids values is one of the most important aspects of parenting. It's how we teach them what we believe and how to behave in any given situation.

Some of my own most closely held values are (in no particular order):

Honesty
Respect
Responsibility
Compassion
Kindness
Integrity
Optimism
Independence
Resilience
Generosity
Community
Friendship
Spirituality
Education
Ambition
Personal growth
Consideration
Love

I could go on and on...

What are yours? They don't have to be the same as mine, **you just need to**

know what yours are and communicate them to your kids.

When we yell at our kids because we are feeling out of control, are we headed toward Mt. Olympus or Mt. Vesuvius? …Vesuvius!

When we teach our kids about being a good friend or even model it by taking a friend some chicken soup when she has a cold, are we headed toward Mt. Olympus or Mt. Vesuvius? …Mt. Olympus!

When a friend hurts our feelings, but we try to see where their hurt comes from, are we headed toward Mt. Olympus or Mt. Vesuvius? …Mt. Olympus!

Get the picture? We can always measure our own behavior and make a decision about it by asking ourselves which mountain we are headed toward at that time.

I have one particular pet peeve; lying. I can't stand it! My friends and family know that I don't ever want to be lied to, and they know they can count on me to tell them the truth, too.

So often, I see parents who tell their kids, "The cookies are all gone!" When, in fact, the cookies are not all gone. The child took a cookie out of the package that still had many cookies remaining. Kids aren't stupid. They know darn well that there are still cookies in there. Now, they think, "Hmmm...Now I know this is an adult I can't trust. I know there are cookies in there. Does she think I'm crazy?" Mt. Vesuvius, here we come!

The real truth is that we want our kids to learn that eating one or two cookies is plenty. We need to teach them reasonableness, and personal responsibility. Most important, we want to teach our kids to speak the truth and to trust that we will speak the truth to them. As they get older, being comfortable telling the truth becomes ever more important as the stakes become higher.

"Ok, let's just have two cookies, because dinner is in an hour and then we're putting the package away so we aren't tempted to eat any more than that. We can have more later after dinner!" Now, that's headed toward Mt. Olympus in the teaching-our-kids-reasonable-boundaries department!

When we are checking our e-mail instead of listening to how our kids' day at school was, is that headed toward Mt. Olympus or Mt. Vesuvius? Ah…this one is a little bit trickier.

Time

Sometimes, we need to take a few minutes away from the kids to take care of our own business. However, it is also important that the kids see we are making it a priority to listen and spend time with them, too. Again, we are modeling the balance of our needs and theirs and we are giving them our undivided attention when we are done taking care of our stuff.

Space

Kids need to learn to respect our space. Walking into a room and demanding our attention is rude. They need to learn to get our attention in a more respectful way. To that end, we as parents need to respect their space. Before walking into a room and demanding that they drop everything to "hurry up and go", we need to give them a minute to finish up what they're doing and transition to the next activity.

Chapter Three

Mirror, mirror on the wall...
Being a good role model

*"Life, like a **mirror**, never gives back more than we put into it"* Anonymous

*"When looking for faults use a **mirror**, not a telescope"* Anonymous

We are who we are not only because we were born this way, but also because of how we were raised by our parents. Our parents are also products of their parents...and so on.

Thinking about how we parent is a relatively new concept. We may be the first generation of parents that actually overly obsesses about how we parent our children. It is truly an unprecedented concept within many families. Until recently, there was not such a microscope put on parenting, and certainly not a library full of books on the do's and don'ts.

We must examine what parts of how we were parented were wonderful and what parts could use some improvement. (No blaming necessary here! Just awareness and making choices.)

Kids become what they see. You are constantly teaching by example, even when you aren't aware of it. Take a look at yourself and your life. What do you think? Would you be proud if your child emulated you?

!!DANGER!!
!!DANGER!!
!!DANGER!!

Taking a good luck at ourselves can be a pretty uncomfortable exercise. You may be tempted to close this book right now and avoid the discomfort of what you see when you look in the mirror and examine your behavior.

I encourage you to push through any discomfort that may arise during this part. Don't give up. In fact, pushing through discomfort is one of the most important tools we can teach our kids!

You've got this!

"MIRROR, MIRROR"

"Do I really sound like that when I'm mad?"

"YIKES!"

"Would I want my son to behave that way?"

"AHHH!"

"Did I just say that to my child?"

"Is there any connection between my whining and my daughter's whining?"

Looking in the mirror requires that we take responsibility for our actions. Once we really take a good look at them, we can choose whether or not to continue those behaviors. That's the good news! Remember the Michael Jackson song, Man in the Mirror?

I'm Starting with The Man In
The Mirror
I'm Asking Him To Change
His Ways
And No Message Could Have
Been Any Clearer
If You Wanna Make The World
A Better Place
Take A Look At Yourself, And
Then Make A Change

Michael Jackson

That's all you should ask of yourself as a parent. Look...recognize...change, if necessary.

The beauty of this exercise of self-reflection is that it makes us more aware. From there we can choose to make a change or not, but without that awareness, nothing can change. That awareness is sometimes painful, but the choices it brings with it are gifts.

Once we are fortunate enough to have kids, the choices we make no longer impact only ourselves. They impact our partners and our kids, too. (MORE PRESSURE!) Our kids pay the price for our unhealthy choices and the resulting chaos that occurs as a result of those choices.

Making a choice to make a change is good for everyone. It always includes a teaching opportunity to instill healthy values and to model the courage it takes to make those improvements and changes.

Making mistakes in front of our kids is of vital importance. I remember at 22 years old realizing for the first time that my parents were human and actually had faults. They fell off of their pedestals! HARD! The realization was both frightening and liberating for me. It gave me permission to make mistakes and to be human – just like them, but it also took a period of grieving to accept them as flawed individuals.

Being Human in Front of Our Kids

We need to model our humanness for our kids and to show them how to make mistakes, how to tolerate the discomfort of living with those mistakes, and most importantly, how to make things better. Sometimes, the best modeling involves admitting that we don't have all of the answers and that we have to employ an expert who can help us. This models resourcefulness – a very important value – and also that we don't have to know it all. We just have to keep going until we figure it out.

In life, we are all faced with challenges:

- Disappointment
- Breakups
- Job loss
- Illness
- Death of a loved one
- Financial stress
- Work stress
- Anxiety
- Depression
- Etc.

The list is never-ending.

The true measure of a person is how he or she stands up to those challenges.

Our children are watching us as we navigate the waters of our challenges.

Kids watch their parents constantly, and much more than you think. They are learning how to navigate through life's many challenges. As the parent, you are their example.

Kid: "Mommy, you're a b*tch!" I ask myself, "Where did she get that?" All too often, one child will see another do something at school and not quite know what to do with it. Then, she brings it home and tries it out on mom and dad. Then, watching her parents' response, she figures she can take that response back to the school yard. These are great teachable moments and are often a good opportunity to teach our kids how to handle difficult peer situations out of experience and compassion. Parents, unfortunately, often miss this teaching opportunity.

When your child misbehaves, ask yourself, how would I want my child to handle this if someone else did it to him?

I challenge you, as I challenge myself, to hold yourself to a higher standard as parents. Pretend as if there is a video camera following you around all of the time. In reality, there <u>are</u> little eyes watching and absorbing!

- Don't let challenges become roadblocks or excuses!
- Turn your challenges into opportunities for growth and learning.

"Parenting Backwards" involves modeling integrity. The very core of integrity means honesty, sincerity, and congruence. Your words need to match your actions. Your words and actions need to match your values. Your values are one of the most important gifts you give to your children.

Do what you say you will do, follow through, be predictable, trustworthy and solid for your kids. This will ensure their sense of safety and security enabling them to comfortably explore the world.

Seeing ourselves through the eyes of others

Parenting in front of other people has always made me a little nervous. I worry about what others might think. Especially since having the nerve to call myself a "parenting expert" really adds the extra pressure!

Many people are self-conscious about their parenting, including me. What if I'm being too harsh? What if I'm being too lenient? What will other people think? Do other people think my kids are brats? What will others think if I lose my temper in public? If my kid has a tantrum in public, will I know how to handle it? Please, God, don't let her have a tantrum in public!!! Ugh...the horror of it all!

As parents, we often have to set our egos aside. How we look to others and what we think others might think of us, must be secondary to what we need to do to raise our kids to be amazing adults. Seizing the teaching opportunity in each moment is more important than trying to avoid feeling foolish.

The best ways I have found to set my ego aside in those horrific moments, is to take a deep breath and think to myself,

- "What is my kid trying to communicate to me?"
- "How can I best teach her the coping mechanisms she needs to get through this?"

These thoughts often get me out of myself, my frustration, my self-consciousness in front of others and my own ego and puts me in a more loving space toward my child.

Chapter 4

Family Life as a Team Sport

"Success comes from knowing that you did your best to become the best that you are capable of becoming." John Wooden

A family is like a sports team

Raising a family is like coaching a sports team. We want to impart the importance of working together, we want to create a culture of togetherness, we want to be there for each other through thick and thin and most of all, we want to be a winning team. So, get your family in a huddle, get your clipboard out and talk team strategy…it might need some adjustment.

We can all envision a championship football team who has just won the Super Bowl. So, what does that look like for a family? Do you have what it takes to bring home the win?

As parents we need to impart our values and teach our kids how to be a member of Team (insert your last name here)! My family is Team Alkazian! Ok, I know it sounds hokey. You don't actually have to use the words if it seems silly to you, but just keep in the back of your mind the values that you want to teach your kids. Just like an athlete needs to understand the fundamentals of his sport, we need to teach our kids our values – the fundamentals of the family.

When the going gets tough, you want your kids to turn to you. When they need something, you want your kids to ask you first. When they aren't sure how to go about handling a situation you want them to look to your values first – not outside the family.

An important component necessary for your kids to turn toward your family for guidance is **safety**. It is this feeling of safety that will help them to come to you in time of trouble. They need to feel as though they will be accepted no matter what they say or do. They need to know that you will be there for them and that they can trust that you always have their back.

When your marriage/relationship affects the whole team

One of the most important ways that kids feel safe is when Mom and Dad's relationship is on solid ground. When Mom and Dad are good, the kids are good. The foundation of the family is based on the strength of your marriage or primary relationship. Kids don't need to worry about the troubles you might be having behind closed doors. If things aren't going well…they know. Little eyes and ears are everywhere.

After even a minor disagreement, my daughter would ask, "Are you and Daddy getting divorced?" She knew other kids' parents who divorced and she often worried about us – thinking that if we aren't solid, everything would come crashing down. Learning to fight fair and to remain respectful through disagreements is so important. If you find yourselves fighting in a way that is hurtful or does damage to the relationship, get some guidance on healthy and respectful fighting. Seek out some marriage counseling to stop the damage and preserve the relationship that your kids need you to take good care of. They are learning how to disagree and how to work things out through your example.

Unconditional Love

The next fundamental in the game plan of the family, is **unconditional love**. When a child knows she is loved no matter how bad her behavior, she feels safe to test the limits and figure out who she is in the context of the family and the context of her greater social group.

Another component of creating your solid team is setting firm, consistent limits and giving kids a sense of responsibility and ownership in the family. Doing chores, taking responsibility for some actions or being helpful around the house makes kids feel a part of the home and the running of the home. That contributes to the feeling of being a part of the team/family.

Giving kids good, firm limits teaches kids their appropriate place in the family and how much space they should take up in the world. Kids who are over-indulged, who are given too many choices and who have too much power in the family are frightened, anxious and act out in an effort to get their parents to take back the power in the family.

Envision your child at each age. At birth their shoulders can't handle any more than eating, sleeping and pooping. That's it! As they get older, they can handle a little more, a little more, and a little more each year. Eventually, our goal is to have a 16 year old who can handle driving a lethal weapon, rising to that enormous responsibility and knowing that the consequences of their actions and choices are in their hands.

What about when parents don't agree?

Often, parents have different styles of parenting based upon their own upbringing, their own experiences, and their own personalities. In fact, **we usually choose our mates for the personality traits that balance our own, though those are the often the reasons that they drive us crazy later on.** As parents, presenting a unified position to our kids is essential, or else we teach them how to play us against each other.

Parents need to polish their communication skills, discuss and listen to each other in order to figure out what their parenting philosophy is and their mission statement so that their decision on how to deal with a given parenting situation can be agreed upon.

When parents have different styles in how they relate to people, it's actually a great thing for kids. They learn how to deal with different temperaments, personalities, and how to communicate effectively. However, this can also be a challenge for parents. It is important not to allow kids to use one parent's personality style against the other in order to get what they want or to avoid what is coming to them. It can be difficult and parents have to watch for their children using those differing styles to deflect from what they have done. For example, a child will misbehave in some way and then get mom and dad to start fighting about how to handle it so the kid can then slip out of the room unnoticed. Mission accomplished! The kid avoided getting in trouble.

How a family spends its time teaches kids what is important.

If you believe in being active and having healthy bodies, then spending the weekends on the couch isn't teaching kids to lead an active lifestyle. If you loved hiking before you had kids, take the kids hiking. If you love building things, teach your kids to build. Share your passions and let teaching them your values motivate you to do the right thing – even when you don't feel like it. Remember, your kids are watching!!!

Extended Family

I always tell my clients to be careful how they treat their parents. Are you patient with your elderly parents or grandparents? Remember, in 30 years, you will be that parent and your kids will have learned how to treat <u>you</u> from watching <u>you</u> now. Remember, your kids are watching!!!

How you and your spouse deal with extended family is also a very important part of how you teach your child to be a member of your team/family. How do you deal with your in-laws? Do you work hard with your spouse to bring the two families together however difficult that may be? Remember, your kids are watching!!!

Modeling respect toward everyone is important, even those with whom you don't agree, whose values differ from your own, or whose lifestyles you wouldn't choose for yourself. Remember, your kids are watching!!! (Annoyed yet?)

All we can say to our parents and in-laws and the generation they grew up in is "we forgive you, respect you and we want to learn from you". We have learned a lot about how to behave and not to behave. We learned how to love and how to be a family, but we also learned what parenting behaviors we don't want to repeat. For instance, if you didn't like it when your parents fought in front of you, then don't fight in front of your kids. If you didn't like a wooden spoon across your fanny (I hope you didn't like it!) then find another way to discipline. If you didn't like the "scream first, ask questions later" craziness, then change that. What things happened in your upbringing that you swore you would never repeat when you became a parent? How often do you catch yourself doing it anyway?!

I know that saying "Just don't do it" seems overly simplistic, but making the decision to be different and to make a different choice is a great first step toward parenting in the right direction.

Pets are members of your team, too!

Raising pets is another way that we teach our kids about the team sport called family. Having a pet brings a family together in a loving way and it doesn't have to be shuttled to sports practices, doesn't need braces and doesn't need a college education. Pets bring so much love into a family and teach our kids about limit setting (a well-trained dog is a happy dog!), they teach about unconditional love, they teach responsibility and eventually they even teach us how to cope with losing them.

When you lose a member of the team

My family recently lost our beloved dog, Havi. We all adored her and she adored us. In fact, I was her "person". When I worked at home, Havi was under my desk and showed her love for me by rubbing against my foot every once in a while. She never once talked back to me! No one else in my house was as happy to see me when I got home as Havi was. When she died, I cried because I lost a friend who loved me 24/7 and who I loved back dearly. Aside from the wonderful years we had together, she also taught our family that we could come together to do something really hard – saying goodbye. We now know that together we can get through something very sad and very difficult. We can survive the hard moments. Havi taught us that through our tears we can still laugh at the funny things we remember – showing us the balance of life and the beauty in the circle of life. What a gift she was in life and even in death. Now, we love our new dogs, Lacey and Jackson. They will never replace our dear Havi, but we love them just the same.

During the rough times in life – and there will be rough times – families have to learn to turn toward each other. Sometimes, in their pain, people will turn away from their families for solace. For example, they will turn toward bad habits and toward other people. As parents, we must model turning toward each other and supporting one another. Even when it's hard to do. Stay with the team no matter what.

The glue that holds us together

The greatest glue that holds a family together are **traditions and rituals**. Rituals can revolve around religion, they can revolve around holidays, or they can simply be something like the weekly ritual of having dinner with Grandma on Sunday nights. Kids love traditions and rituals because they are a constant in their life that is safe and that they can look forward to and count on.

Baking your kids' favorite holiday cookies, for example, creates memories and a comfortable feeling when year after year during the holidays, those same smells are present and the same tastes that remind them of great times spent together. One year, my kids and I were putting up our Hanukkah decorations and my oldest daughter, Lauren, remembered a particular sparkly menorah we had hung up the previous year from our entry light fixture. She asked where it was because she loved it and wanted it right back where it was the year before! Voila, a ritual is born and the glue in our family just got a little bit stronger.

Chapter 5

Teaching coping skills – the backbone of lifelong success

Emotional Intelligence in Parenting

"AAAAHHHHHH!!!!!!!"

Who hasn't heard that in their house recently? I know I have! It could have been me, my husband or any one of my kids.

So many moments in life are "AAAAHHHHHH!!!" moments. It might be when I stubbed my toe after leaving my own shoe in the middle of the floor. How about when I fell getting into my car the other morning? My rear end didn't think it was so funny, but my kids sure did!

How about the frustrations of life when things don't go our way? We have to be able to handle any and all of these types of moments. We have to maintain the presence of mind to get through the moments, problem-solve to fix whatever happened and cope with the hurt, sadness, disappointment or pain that results. Kids, too, need to learn to put problems in their proper place. Some problems require more emotional energy and, more often than not, they require less.

Emotion Coaching (adapted from *Raising an Emotionally Intelligent Child* by Dr. John Gottman and enhanced by me!)

Teaching our kids about their feelings and appropriate expression of those feelings is one of the most important gifts we can give them. It is the cornerstone of Emotional Intelligence (E.Q.) and many people believe that a high E.Q. is more predictive of success in life than a high I.Q.

Teaching these skills to our kids is very hard for many parents because they don't always have a grip on their own feelings, let alone, have the ability to teach what it's all about. When I work with parents, I'm often amazed as I watch parents learn about their own feelings as they travel the journey of teaching their children how to deal with theirs.

Here are the steps:

Step 1. Label the feeling

The first step in understanding feelings is identifying what feeling is actually being experienced.

Angry/mad
Sad
Disappointed
Hurt
Scared
Frustrated
Excited
Etc…

For younger kids, their feelings are literal aches and pains in their bodies.

After his friend cancelled his play date, a little boy might feel a strange sensation in his stomach and he knows it feels terrible, but he doesn't know that it's called disappointment. He just knows that it feels yucky and that he has to get rid of it somehow. Our job is to build a bridge from his stomach to his brain telling him that what he is feeling is called disappointment. That way, in the future, when he feels that same sensation, he will say, "Hey, I know this! It's called disappointment and I have the tools to make it go away or put it in its proper place."

Step 2. Acknowledge the feeling

Once a kid knows what his feeling is called, he wants to know that he's not crazy for feeling this way and that you understand what he's going through. We need to normalize it for our kids.

"I don't blame you for feeling disappointed. You were really looking forward to having that play date."

That validation and compassion tells your child that you really get it, and that it's ok to feel the way he does.

We can also normalize those feelings by telling them that we have also felt that way many times. This adds to the validation of their feelings. We're saying:

"I totally get what you're going through. I've felt that way many times, too!"

Relating our own personal story and how we got through it is always good. It lets our kids see that we are human.

Step 3. Limit-setting – The Do's and Don'ts

Now that our little boy knows what he's feeling and that his feelings are justified and understood, he needs to know what to do with them. All he knows is that it still feels really uncomfortable in his stomach area. What to do? He knows that punching his sister in the face would take some of the tension out of his body, but he also knows that he'll get in big trouble for that one. He needs to know what his options are and what to avoid.

"I get that you're feeling very disappointed, but we don't hit! (what <u>not</u> to do)
"You need to use your words!" (what <u>to</u> do)
"Say, Mommy, I'm so sad that my friend isn't coming over!" (what to say instead of hitting)
"C'mon, let's go take the dog for a walk (go for a run, stomp around the backyard – some type of tension release) and figure out what we can do today instead."

Adults can certainly relate to this, too. Don't you ever go for a walk to blow off steam? Works much better than kicking the poor dog!

Step 4. Values Infusion

When setting limits with kids, this is a perfect time to stick in a lesson in values.

Keep in mind what your values are:

Kindness
Compassion
Respect
Responsibility
Honesty
Patience
Etc…

For example:

"We don't hit! That's not <u>nice</u>!"
"Biting hurts people. We only bite food, <u>not people</u>."
"Leaving your clothes on the bathroom floor isn't <u>respectful</u> to the next person who uses it."
"Throwing toys hurts people and property. You're showing me that you can't be <u>respectful</u> with that toy." (Take the toy a way for a period of time)

Step 5. Recovery

A small hang nail might elicit a two-minute tirade, but anything longer might be a bit excessive. It is our job to teach our kids how long each emotional reaction is appropriately expressed. Big things may require TLC for a longer amount of time. Small issues should require less time and less drama. Think about the Universal Pain Scale. Is this difficulty a 5? Then, the reaction is warranted for X amount of time. Not too little, but not too much either. Our kids sometimes need us to remind them of when enough is enough. Remember though, our kids are watching how we respond to frustration and disappointment and are learning from us constantly and copying our good and not-so-good reactions. It's ok to say to your child, "This ouchie is a 2 and you're screaming like it's a 9. Let's turn it down and go do something else." Remember, though, that what may seem little to you might feel big to the child. Be compassionate and open to the possibility that your child may also need to cry about something else and is using this little ouchie as a way to release some feelings that need to get out.

Taking our kids through these steps over and over again as they experience the bumps along the road of life will eventually teach them that feelings have names, the feelings are normal and that there is an appropriate way to express those feelings, which will often give some relief from the discomfort of the feeling.

The test I often use when deciding what tools to teach my kids in dealing with their uncomfortable emotions, I ask this question:

"What would I want them to do 30 years from now when they experience this feeling at work or with their spouses?"

For example, when my daughter is frustrated later in life, it would be appropriate to go for a run or a bike ride to release some of that tension, give her some time to think, put things into perspective and give her a healthy outlet. So, today, I might say, let's run around the backyard together or let's grab your bike and ride down to the corner and back.

Sometimes, leaving the situation won't be an option and I'll want her to be able to handle herself and her feelings in other ways. Sometimes, I suggest taking some deep breaths, drawing a picture, writing in a journal or on a white board. Again, we're honoring the feelings and giving them a chance to be expressed, but still remaining respectful of other people and property.

Tolerating Discomfort

One of the hardest emotional obstacles that I find with my clients is the ability for the parents to **tolerate their child's discomfort**. In truth, it makes a lot of sense why this is hard.

When we bring these little babies home from the hospital, they are so helpless and dependent. It is our job to comfort them and take away any discomfort they may have. At that age, it is hunger, a wet diaper, a gas bubble or the dire need for a nap (that one I SO understand).

Our job is to take away that discomfort as quickly as possible and we are instantly rewarded by the quieting of the baby's cries. Here's the catch: after the first year of life, then our job isn't always to comfort them. Cruel joke, huh?

**Sometimes, our kids need to feel a
little bit of discomfort in order to
learn how to grow up on the inside**.

Growing character often takes some
tough love. Yes, our kids continue to
need our comfort, but they also have to
learn to wait, to delay their gratification,
to fall down and learn that they can get
back up, and that their actions have
consequences in order to grow up.
Most important, in order to learn to get
through the rough times in life, they
need to have some rough times, fight
through them, push themselves past
their comfort zone, and come out the
other end having survived and hopefully
learned that they can get through
anything.

Anxiety is a common experience that
everyone has to some degree. In many
situations, anxiety is actually helpful.
For example, they have done studies
that show that students who experience
a low to moderate level of anxiety when
taking a test actually do better than the
students with no anxiety or a great deal
of anxiety. Interesting. Thankfully, this
proves that anxiety isn't all bad, but
when it gets to high levels, too much of
a good thing is no longer a good thing.

Many kids today are experiencing extreme levels of anxiety. More kids than ever are on anti-anxiety medication. As parents, it's is our job to alleviate as much anxiety as possible, and to teach our kids the tools they need to manage, reduce and cope with anxiety.

"Do not let yesterday take up too much of today." John Wooden

Anxiety actually happens when we leave this moment and begin worrying about either the past or the future. In the present, most of the time, all is well. When we worry about "what will happen when..." we leave this moment and get anxious. Why? Because we have no control over the future. A perceived lack of control is usually what causes anxiety and a lack of confidence that we can handle what will come our way as a result. Now, how does this connect with parenting, you might ask?

Poor limits = anxiety

When we give our kids too many choices, or we allow them too much freedom or we don't set enough limits to show them when they have gone too far with their behavior, our kids experience anxiety. It's as if we handed the reins of the horse to the kids and said, "Have at it!" They're young and inexperienced. How about if we are flying a plane and say to our kids, "Ok, I'm tired. I'm going to take a nap. You fly the plane for a little while." They would be terrified! Though they can't articulate it, this is what it feels like to kids when we don't maintain our authority and power in the relationship with our kids.

In fact, kids will actually behave as though they want more power or control. Right? They try to take over, get cranky when they don't get their way, etc... In reality, they are testing us! They are saying, "I'm going to try this again. Now show me that I DON'T have as much power as I think I do." The more power-hungry kids seem, the more they are begging for us to take the power away from them. Don't you just love the ironies of parenting? Ugh!

The most common way that I see parents giving their power away is engaging in power struggles with their kids. How many days have you gone to bed completely exhausted and feeling as though you've been fighting with your

kids all day? In truth, you <u>should</u> be
exhausted! You have literally been in
the boxing ring. This is not only
exhausting, it is scary for the kids and
incredibly frustrating for the parents
because they feel ineffectual as parents
and just want their kids to do what they
say!

Get out of the boxing ring!

Getting into the boxing ring with your
kids also does something that few
parents are aware of. It levels the
playing field in terms of the relationship.
There is no longer the appropriate
hierarchy of authority. Parent and child
become peers and have to fight it out for
the power in the relationship.
Unfortunately, just by entering the
boxing ring, as a parent you are already
at a disadvantage and are likely to lose
your power to your child. If this
happens, don't get back in the ring! The
more you get in the ring, the more
anxious your child becomes and the
more he will test you and around and
around it goes. Hold your ground! Take
back the heavyweight title!

Here are some helpful words to assist
you in staying out of the boxing ring with

your child and maintaining your parental authority in the family:

- "I'm not interested in fighting with you!"
- "I love you too much to fight with you about this."
- "Let me know when you're ready to…"
- "I hear that you really want to…, but it's my job to make sure that you…"

Avoiding the Rabbit Hole

Sometimes when our kids are "melting down" (for lack of a better way to describe it – but, you know what I'm talking about) we, as parents, have a meltdown of our own. Picture this: Your child is having a tantrum in the middle of the store. Kicking, screaming, the usual horrors that we dread when going into public. We feel at a loss to know what to do to stop the tantrum, we are incredibly embarrassed that this is happening in public and want to crawl under a rock or pretend we've never seen this child before in our lives. What happens then? We finally get them in the car and we start to have a tantrum ourselves. Screaming at them to stop screaming! Now it's a test of wills and a contest to see who can scream the loudest.

This is what I call "Rabbit Hole" behavior. Remember Alice in Wonderland? She follows the rabbit all through the meadow and eventually down the rabbit hole, not knowing how to get back home again. Rather than following our kids down the rabbit hole of behavior, let's attempt to maintain our ability to teach our kids some coping skills. The best way to do this is to see yourself rather than falling down the rabbit hole, sitting along side it and waiting patiently for your child to climb back out to you. Here are some things you can say to your child while he is having a tantrum:

- "I can see that you're having a hard time. I'll just sit here and wait until you're ready to calm down."

Remember, you can tell anyone staring at you that "Yes, this is my child and I'm having a teachable moment, thank you very much!"

Sometimes our kids need help to calm their bodies down when they've fallen so far down the rabbit hole.

- "Do you need my help to calm down? When you stop screaming I'll be happy to hold you." A hug can go a long way toward teaching a child to calm his body down.

In fact, I often tell parents that **the more out-of-control your child becomes, the more calm you should become**. That's a hard thing to do, but with some practice, you'd be surprised how remaining calm will shorten your child's tantrum rather than adding fuel to the fire.

More about E.Q. – Emotional Intelligence

We have to teach our kids to deal with their emotions. They weren't born onto this planet knowing how to handle it all. Dealing with feelings is a new experience and we have to build a bridge for them from their bellies, where the physical sensations of their emotions reside, to their brains that enable them to know what those sensations mean and how to intelligently deal with those feelings.

Giving kids these tools enables them to handle the rough spots in life. It's easy to prepare kids for the good days they'll have as adults, but what about the rough ones?

I'll never forget being 18 years old and finding out that my first boyfriend was going out with one of my friends. I was devastated. Ok, I know now that it was just puppy love, but at the time I thought I was the Juliet to his Romeo. I ate myself into oblivion and I stayed in bed every minute I could. I barely functioned through the day and experienced what I now know was depression.

Now, we'll never be able to take the sting and hurt out of a break up for our kids, but giving them the tools and confidence to deal with their pain is the gift we can give them. We can teach them that they can get back on their feet after a devastating blow.

Worse than a silly breakup with a high school sweetheart, are the inevitable real tragedies that life sometimes hands us. Illness, accidents and the death of a loved one are likely to happen to all of us at one time or another. In fact, it is the cycle of life that we will eventually bury our parents. It's a sad thought, but the part I want you to consider here is that your children will eventually bury you. (Am I talking about death again? It figures!)

Our ultimate goal is to give our kids the coping skills to handle the feelings and logistics of losing us, or someone else they love dearly.

One of the best ways to teach our kids good coping skills is, of course, to model it. When things don't go the way you want, how do you react? Remember, your kids are always watching you and absorbing information. This doesn't mean that you can't cry in front of your kids, in fact, showing your kids that you can cry and still be ok is a very important lesson.

Crying is how we show sadness. Be mindful, of course, not to be scary when YOU cry. Kids get scared when they see their parents sad. We are their rocks, so when their rocks are weak, they wonder "who will be strong for me and take care of me?" We can show strength with our tears. Let them know that we are sad and that it's an appropriate feeling given the situation. It's even ok to give them a task to feel helpful. For example, asking for a hug will make everyone feel better. You, because you need it, and the child because he will then feel useful in a helpless moment. Be careful, of course, not to cross the line and require your child to take care of you. We all still need to be able to take care of ourselves, or when we can't we need to elicit the help of other <u>adults</u> to care for us. If it is appropriate, tell your child why you are sad. Share your feelings. This will help your child feel more connected to you and will show them that sharing feelings and talking things through is important.

"What doesn't kill us makes us stronger."

Ok, so how do we teach our kids to tolerate the aches and pains of life?

The first thing we do is model for them how to tolerate the pain of daily life. We need to share with them when we have a bad day, talk about what happened and talk about our plans to get through it. Then, we need to follow up afterward and talk about what worked and what didn't work.

I know that this is hard for a lot of people. For many of us, when we are struggling with a challenge, we prefer to go into our caves and lick our wounds until we figure out what to do about it. That's ok, if that's your style. I've been known to do this, at times, too. It's my hope to encourage you to share your discomfort with your kids, talk about your inclination to want to go into your cave and then what you chose to do to solve your problem when you came out of your cave. Even young kids can learn a lot about life around the dinner table when mom and dad share their thoughts and feelings. Let them see how you are supportive of one another.

It is, of course, important not to over share if things are scary. If you have a very sensitive child, you don't want to cause them more anxiety than necessary. Perhaps, in that case, you can discuss what happened after the fact and how things turned out, rather than burdening your frightened child with adult-sized worries.

Very young children, also don't know about the challenges of daily life. It's ok to share with little ones that you felt sad at work today or that you're working on a "puzzle to solve at work". Bringing your feelings and struggles to the family dinner table and speaking in their language with an eye on the teaching opportunities, lets kids know that life isn't perfect, but that mom and dad are working on it and all will be well.

Modeling this as kids grow up teaches them that every day isn't all good. It gives them a more realistic view that each day has its joys and challenges.

By the way, don't forget to share the joys of your days, too! Let them know you saw a beautiful sunset on your way home from work or you saw the colors of the changing leaves on the trees in the neighborhood. I always love to tell my daughters about something kind that someone did for me unexpectedly. Sharing those "good deeds for the day" is important and shows that there is kindness in our world, too.

Over-Indulgence with Pain Avoidance

After modeling, parents need to allow their kids to experience their own discomforts. Don't protect them from every bump, skinned knee or hurt feeling. Most important, **DON'T BE AFRAID OF YOUR CHILD'S PAIN**. That is one of the most common ways that I see parents over-indulge their kids. Protecting them from pain robs kids of the opportunities to learn how to get through the rough spots in life. Ever heard of "helicopter parents"? Danger...danger...!

How many times have you heard of parents blaming the school when their child is in trouble? Of course, there are exceptions, but as parents we should be asking what did my child do to invite this chaos? Even if he was an innocent bystander, we need to teach our kids about the consequences of choosing the wrong friends and the concept of "guilty by association" rather than getting them out of trouble or shielding them from the issues at hand.

As parents of younger kids you may be thinking, "Oh, this doesn't apply to me yet", but in reality, who our children choose as friends begins as soon as they are in any type of school or social setting. Certain kids are attractive to our kids and many kids will begin patterns that will continue into their school-age and teen years. As our kids start to have play dates, they begin to see how other family teams work or don't work. We need to be overseeing these friendships from a very young age and commenting when we hear our values being violated. For example, if we hear two kids talking about a third kid in a negative light, we need to make a comment. "How would you like it if someone spoke about you that way?" "It isn't kind to talk disrespectfully about other people." This is a great teaching opportunity to share your values about gossip or talking behind others' backs.

Anger is one of the most difficult emotions for kids to handle. Let's get real, most adults don't handle anger very well either. In fact, some of the most mild-mannered people in their day to day lives will be the biggest road ragers. Why? Anger is the emotion that while we might be able to push it away, hold it off for another day or even convince ourselves that we're sad instead, it can be very sneaky. It will leak out when we least expect it. Anger will show its ugly little teeth when we are only mildly irritated. We might act like we have been brutally attacked, leaving those around us wondering what they were missing.

Depression is believed to be "anger turned inward"

When we feel angry, but don't feel safe enough to express it directly or at all, we will swallow it and hold onto it and even become angry at ourselves for feeling this way. In many people this will display itself as depression because it's safer to take our anger out on ourselves than on those with whom we are really angry. It's difficult for most adults. When children experience this, it is especially difficult if not impossible for them to understand what is happening.

Of course, taking our anger out on ourselves isn't the best option. I hope that if this sounds familiar and is something you are battling, please consult a professional therapist to learn healthier ways to express your anger and clear out the cob webs that might be haunting you or causing you to self-medicate with alcohol, drugs, food, etc. You will be a better parent if you are willing to look honestly at it!

Once your own emotional closets are cleared out, it makes it much easier to educate your kids about their feelings. Let's not perpetuate your family's knack for stuffing feelings inside or expressing feelings inappropriately. With your own kids, you can begin to teach new emotional tools that you may not ever have been taught.

Anger is a normal and healthy emotion that everyone experiences. The key is knowing what to do with it when it arises. Remember, no ugly teeth!

Anger is actually another emotion plus energy.

FEAR + energy = anger
SADNESS + energy = anger

When our kids become angry – which is so easy for kids to tap into – we have to be ok with their anger. Many of us grew up with the unspoken rule that it isn't ok to express anger. Or, conversely, some families display too much anger.   Anger becomes the default emotion for all emotions and makes some people not want to express anger at all.

In order for us, as parents, to teach our kids the appropriate expression of anger, we have to examine our own relationship with anger.

- What were the rules around anger in your family growing up?
- What did you learn about anger and its expression?
- Are your expressions of anger appropriate for the situations?
- What do you wish your kids knew about anger that you didn't when you were a kid?
- If anger is hard for you and you know that your interpretations are a bit distorted, get some help from a professional on how to express and teach anger appropriately in your family.

The best and most important way that our kids learn what anger is and how it's supposed to look is by watching us.

- We want our kids to know that anger is a normal and healthy emotion.
- We want our kids to know when is and isn't the time to let others know we are feeling angry.
- We want our kids to know when it is appropriate to express our anger to others and how to do so in a way that is respectful.
- We want our kids to know that they can assert themselves and ask for what they need without having to shame or insult others.

Again, using the E.Q. tools we discussed earlier, teaching our kids about anger is a big and long-term job. It's a very complex emotion and each developmental stage brings with it new challenges and reasons to be angry.

What to say:

"I can see that you are really angry at that toy! It's just not cooperating, is it?" "I don't blame you for being angry! You really wanted it to work and were so looking forward to playing with it." "It's ok to be angry and to use your words or even ask for help, but throwing the toy isn't going to solve your problem."

Embarrassment

Ok, I already said that anger is one of the most difficult emotions to process and express, but in reality, embarrassment is THE most difficult of them all. All of our emotions are housed and stored in our internal organs. This actually makes it fairly easy to push down, ignore and hold off those feelings if we find it necessary. We store it like a squirrel might store acorns for the winter.

Embarrassment, however, is housed in the brain. Having the discomfort of embarrassment – and I do mean discomfort! – without any place to put it because it's just hanging out front and center in the brain gives us no outlet and no escape. There it is right there as if everyone can see it. Feeling that sense of total exposure is so painful. We need to really give our kids the tools mentioned earlier in this chapter in a very concrete way to help them know what to do in these brutal moments.

What to say:

"I know you are really embarrassed!" "I
don't blame you! Anyone would be
embarrassed in that situation."
"Being embarrassed feels so terrible, I
know! I've been there many times, too."
"Rather than yelling and screaming, let's
go outside and take a breather and
you'll feel better when you calm down."

One of the most important aspects in
teaching our kids to tolerate all of these
uncomfortable emotions is not to fix it or
make it better for them. They need to
learn that they will recover from these
internal "skinned knees" just like they do
the external ones.

Many parents will fix the situation in an effort to make their child feel better, but that's not actually doing their child any favors. Labeling the feeling, acknowledging their experience and giving them tools to deal with the feeling gives kids the tools they will need when mom and dad aren't around to fix things. If parents make the problems go away in an effort to alleviate their child's emotional pain, the child doesn't learn how to get through it himself.

Allow your kids to learn how to tolerate their own discomfort. If Mom and Dad can stand to watch their child in some discomfort for a short time, then the child will be increasingly able to withstand the pain.

Convey Confidence

Even better yet, if mom and dad not only tolerate the child's discomfort, but also stand by with full confidence that all will be well, the child will feel that confidence as he processes his feelings, expresses himself and works through it. Most important, when he recovers from it, he will have the sense of mastery and pride in having accomplished something important.

What? I already mentioned tolerating our kids' discomfort in this chapter? I did? Of course, I did! In fact, I'm likely to mention it again and again. That's how important I think this topic is! Thank you for indulging me this repetition, but that's how kids and adults learn best. Frankly, if you remember nothing else from the experience of reading this book, please remember this:

WHEN YOU CAN TOLERATE YOUR KIDS' DISCOMFORT, YOU WILL GIVE THEM THE GREATEST GIFT OF THEIR LIVES – THE ABILITY TO TOLERATE DISCOMFORT THEMSELVES! (Yes, I just screamed! That's how important I think this is! You've heard it previously in this book and I can promise you that you'll hear it again!)

"The only thing we have to fear is fear itself." Franklin D. Roosevelt

"Love is what we were born with, fear is what we learned here." Unknown

Fear is a normal part of growing up. Aw, heck, fear is a normal part of daily life! For some kids, fear is the theme for each and every day. Think about it, the reason the network news is so popular is because people not only want to be informed, people want the gory details. Americans, especially, feed off of the gruesome details of crime, war and the general misfortune of others because they feel a sense of control over things that make them feel fearful when they know more information about it.

There are several periods in which fear is a hallmark of that developmental stage. As kids begin to realize that the world is bigger than they had previously understood, they begin to get frightened and need to touch base with their parents more often. For example, when little ones begin to walk and realize that they have the capability of traveling farther away from mommy than ever before, they tend to become clingy and more anxious until they get settled and comfortable with their new-found power within the new developmental phase.

More than ever before, we are seeing kids experiencing excessive amounts of fear and anxiety. Anxiety is also often accompanied by depression. As parents, we need to give our kids more tools to handle these fears and the challenges that go along with them. When it goes beyond what you can do, do not hesitate to offer them some professional counseling to give them the necessary skills to push through their fears and feel confident in themselves. Consider the inroads that are being created in their brains. Those pathways will likely be the pathways set down for the duration of their lives and can't be changed without concerted effort.

Pushing our kids to do things that are scary for them works for some, but not at all for other kids. Highly sensitive kids do better when offered the opportunity to observe, consider, contemplate and bow out, if necessary. Given that opportunity repeatedly, sensitive kids are more likely to engage, but forcing them can push them the other way toward avoidance, trauma and total resistance. (More about parenting sensitive kids in the next chapter.)

The greatest depression-buster we know is optimism.

When we give our kids the tools to overcome adversity with hope that things will get better, faith that they won't always feel this way and trust in the process of growth and progress, we have then equipped

**them with all that they need to get
through the toughest of times.**

"Choosing happiness" is a concept that
many people never learn. If we teach
our kids that they are the masters of
their feelings and their feelings are not
the rulers of them, we give them a gift
that they can take into their adult lives
and utilize on a daily basis.

Many adults today don't even know this
concept. So often, we walk around this
planet reacting to our feelings. When
something happens that we don't like,
we are cranky about it all day or even all
week! How about shifting perspective
on that same scenario and seeing it as a
clarifying message or a blessing in
disguise? At the very least, decide not
to react. Just observe, acknowledge
and don't let anything ruin your day!
You are in control of that decision 100%.
Instead of being run by our feelings, the
real truth is that actions come first and
feelings follow. We can't do wait to do
something when the feeling arises, we
have to do something and the feelings
will follow! Teach that to your kids!

Chapter Six

When Kids are Hard to Love

"If you have never been hated by your child, you have never been a parent." Bette Davis

Some kids are especially challenging to raise. I always find it a good exercise to reflect back on how easy or difficult you were to raise. Now be honest, here… were you a pleaser or a fighter? Did you go with the flow or were you constantly swimming upstream?

It's an unspoken truth for many parents to admit that they don't always <u>like</u> their child. Some kids actually make themselves <u>unlovable</u> with their behavior. The message here is that you will always love your children…you just might not always like them and it's ok to admit it.

The child who doesn't listen…the child who rages…the child who cries about everything…the child who does unthinkable behaviors (lying, cheating, stealing…). Hard to like!

When we decide to have children, we often have romantic notions of how it will be to be a parent. Our visions of our kids are nearly perfect. We dream of tossing a ball together or going shopping and dressing our little girls up like princesses. We never envision a child who is unruly, impossible, hard to be with and utterly distasteful.

Some parents have confessed to me in my office, often through their tears, that they actually dislike their child. That's a terrible feeling for any parent to feel and even harder to admit. The truth is that some kids make themselves very hard to love.

There is no shame in admitting to yourself that you don't always love your child. The test is simply to use that as a barometer that something is wrong and needs serious attention and to know that you are not alone.

Sometimes, the message is that we need to look at our own baggage. Maybe our child's behavior reminds us of some very dysfunctional family relationship and it makes us not want to look at it.

Of course, when it involves our kids, we MUST look at it. There's no burying our heads in the sand where our kids are concerned. Be courageous and look your fears square in the face. Face them so that your kids can face theirs too, and so that you can all get the help necessary to improve relationships and overall functioning.

"Love me when I least deserve it, because that's when I really need it."
Swedish Proverb

What do we do when the child we live with is not someone we like very much or very often?

When I was training as a therapist, I had a difficult time connecting with one of my clients. I struggled to find something about her that I liked. Thanks to my amazing supervisor at the time, I was finally able to connect with her. My supervisor reminded me that if I was struggling to find something loveable about this person, others probably were, too. In that moment, I was able to feel compassion for my client and develop a very deep and growth-filled relationship (for us both!). I learned to view and understand the world from her perspective.

The same is true for our kids. In most cases, when our kids are hard for us to love, they are likely to have fallen into a pattern of behavior that brings them negative attention. They get used to getting their share of love and attention with bad behavior or even just by being annoying. They don't care if you're yelling, at least you're focusing on them. That's good enough in their minds.

The only way to turn the tides of this pattern is to not be willing to give them our negative attention. When our kids are being annoying, let them know that you'd love to give them attention when they're done with the annoying behavior. That way, you're not feeding the behavior you don't like, but you're also saying that you're happy to give them loving attention when they ask for it appropriately.

Our challenging kids may also struggle socially – not knowing how to be with others or even (or especially) how to be with themselves. This is when they need our love most of all.

At one point, my daughter and I were struggling (in the early teen years) to get along and to find a way to understand each other. I remember sitting down in my bedroom one day with my journal and just started writing (and crying). I wrote these words:

"I'M GOING TO LOVE YOU THROUGH IT!"

In that moment, I was hurt and angry at my daughter, but more important; I was discouraged because I didn't understand her. What I needed to do was love her even more as she was struggling, too. I was the adult and I needed to carry the light for both of us to navigate through the rough terrain we were traveling.

It's when they are most unlovable that they need our love the most!

If you have a child with especially challenging behaviors, you must seek professional help. If not only for your child, for yourself, too. Kids never misbehave for no reason. (I know that was a double negative) They are trying to communicate with us at all times with their behavior. The uglier their behavior, the more pain they are in.

As the adults, we must listen to their behavior, not so much their words,

(unless they are truly able to articulate their pain – which is rare) and seek the help they need and the help **we** need to know how to help them in the best ways!

Highly Sensitive Kids

Some kids are highly sensitive. What does that mean? This group of kids feel the same things that you and I do, they just feel it stronger, deeper, and more pronounced. These kids may be seen as "drama queens", "cry-babies", exaggerators, etc… To them, the cool breeze feels **cold**, the stubbed toe is most certainly broken, the hangnail is a 10 on the universal pain scale and the hurt feelings feel like a mortal wound.

In reality, it really feels that way to them! Trying to reason them out of their discomfort is very unlikely to be helpful.

The best way to help a highly sensitive child is to have compassion for them and support them through their pain and discomfort, while teaching them the coping skills to handle things themselves.

Honestly, I could go on and on about HSK's, but there have been other books written on this subject. Raising highly sensitive kids takes a boat load of compassion and patience.

The most important thing to remember is not to push highly sensitive kids into situations that they do not want to enter (such as birthday parties, roller coasters, etc...you know, the negotiable ones) and honor them to know what they can and cannot handle. They are likely to grow up well as long as they are **not shamed** for being the sensitive souls that they are. In fact, I'm pretty sure that some of the world's greatest artists, musicians, writers and other creative geniuses were and are highly sensitive people. It's not all bad, it's just a gift that comes along with a bit of a curse. **LOVE THEM THROUGH IT!!**

Brain Differences

There are other issues that cause kids to have challenging behaviors such as mood disorders, sensory processing challenges, developmental disorders, and other brain differences. We are all wired differently and it's what makes us all individuals.

If I could give parents of kids with brain differences just a small pearl of wisdom it's to keep in mind the *Parenting*

Backwards philosophy. These challenges can be seen as gifts in that kids have to find creative ways to compensate for their challenges. This has the potential to teach kids to turn "lemons into lemonade" and to see that their challenges and the fight to overcome those challenges will give them strength and wisdom that kids without challenges may never gain.

As their parents, we have the responsibility to teach our kids all that they need to lead healthy and happy adult lives. For kids with challenges, that includes how to get through the rough spots and deal with what challenges them now and as adults.

The greatest gift we can give our kids is never giving up on them. If they see that we aren't giving up on them, they will be able to persevere and never give up on themselves, even when they may want to.

Hang in there and get the help and support every family member may need!

Kids with Anxiety

The most common issue, by far, that I
see in my Parent Coaching practice is
parents helping their kids to deal with
profound anxiety.

Anxiety shows up differently for each
child:

- anger /rage
- worrying
- obsessions
- separation anxiety
- tics
- tantrums
- sleep issues
- school anxiety
- bullying
- and more…

For many families, these anxiety-related
behaviors can hold everyone hostage
and create the need for a family to tip-
toe around the anxious child for fear of
creating yet another big blow-up.

Though the symptoms are incredibly
unlovable behaviors, the truth is that
these kids are simply showing their pain
in the only ways they know how to do
so.

The key to helping these kids is to:

- reduce their anxiety whenever possible
- stay present (if it's safe) to alleviate the possibility of exacerbating any potential separation anxiety
- Don't attempt to discipline them. It only adds more anxiety which fuels the fire.
- Keep in mind they are in pain and the distasteful behavior is the only way they can think to express it.
- Give them tools to express their anxiety in a healthier way; using words.
- Teach tools that will help them to reduce their anxiety for life, for example, exercise, journaling, drawing, deep breathing, yoga, etc...

Kids with anxiety need loving support, even when they're acting in unlovable ways. Avoid the inclination to discipline their behavior and rather address the feelings and give tools for appropriate expression. This will build a warm and deep relationship and enable healing through your loving compassion.

Chapter Seven

Don't be afraid to say "no"!

Setting limits and boundaries

"I guess the real reason that my wife and I had children is the same reason that Napoleon had for invading Russia: it seemed like a good idea at the time." Bill Cosby

The baby is crying. You're both sick and tired of getting up during the night, night after night. You've decided to let the baby cry it out. The pediatrician tells you it's time. Your friends tell you how easy it is. Here you are, thinking you're about to go crazy if you have to listen to another minute of your baby crying. You and your spouse are about to kill each other if one of you doesn't go get the baby. It's not pretty and you know that if you go get the baby, you'll be setting back the clock on sleep training by what seems like years. The dilemma becomes: do I save myself by teaching my baby to sleep through the night or do I save my marriage by going to get the baby to end the tension and torture?

I often tell parents that the first opportunity we have to define our relationship with our kids is through sleep training. It doesn't have to be painful or cruel, but when we teach our children when and where to sleep, we are, for the first time, saying to them "I'm the parent and I know better for you than you know for yourself." If it were up to many babies, they'd stay up all night for fear of missing a party. As adults, we know that our children need lots of sleep because they are growing at a very rapid pace. Plus, we need them to sleep to give us a break. (I hope it's ok to admit that out loud.) A tired parent, is not a happy parent!

Setting limits and boundaries with our kids is absolutely essential in order for them to feel safe and secure as they grow up. Not only do we have to set those limits, we also have to follow through with them and be consistent with them. Then, kids sleep more soundly because they know that their world is predictable and safe. It also prevents anxiety when kids know that the adult decisions are covered by you and they are free to explore, blossom and develop as they're supposed to!

What limits are we supposed to be setting?

Limit-setting with our kids involves teaching them how to behave appropriately in all situations. We have to teach our kids how to behave in public, how to be respectful of others, how to express themselves appropriately, etc… If we see disciplining our children as **teaching**, we are likely to have more patience with the process.

Why do kids test the limits?

Have you ever had to read your child a book over and over and over again until you wished you could unzip your body, step out of it and go running from the house? This is a great example of how kids learn from repetition. The more times we repeat something, the more comfortable our kids will feel about it. In addition, neural pathways in the brain are created by repetition. When kids learn concepts, words, thoughts, feelings, etc… over and over again it creates a connection in their brains that helps it all make sense to them. It also makes kids feel safe and secure to have mom and dad respond in the same ways over and over. This contributes to their ability to predict the big, overwhelming and crazy worlds they live in.

Why do bad behaviors get worse?

I often tell the parents with whom I work that **any behavior that is fed will grow!** Like a flowering plant, if you give it plant food, water it and make sure it gets plenty of sunshine, it is likely to flourish beautifully!

Pouring your attention on an undesired behavior is just like pouring that plant food on it and negative attention is just as potent as positive attention. Another metaphor I like to use is the alley cat. Any behavior you don't like should not be fed – just like an alley cat. Only feed the ones you want to stick around!

The best antidote to a behavior that you don't like is to completely ignore it! Sometimes, we have to address bad behaviors and set limits, though. When setting limits on a behavior that you don't like, do your best to remove all emotion from your interactions. It's the emotion behind our words that becomes the Miracle Grow that feeds the behavior! Stay as neutral as possible.f gffaxzxzaAAXZAQAAAX\ Zaszz1x1azaa112

Reality Parenting

In teaching our kids how to be in this world I believe in recreating real-world scenarios, so that our lessons have long-term application for our kids. I call this "Reality Parenting".

"Reality Parenting" is about teaching our kids what the potential consequences are of their choices. Enter logical consequences. Rather than punishing our kids when they don't behave in a way that is appropriate, we need to teach them how we would prefer that they behave. Even if we know that they know better, we need to stay in the teaching mode. Having our heads spin around with smoke coming out of our ears because they have dashed our expectations is an unwise choice.

When our kids "act out" (defined as: behave in a way that we don't care for, isn't appropriate, embarrasses us and violates our values) we want the consequences of their actions to have a **direct connection to those actions**. For example, if your child hits another child, he should be removed from the room. We also have to let the child know that he has violated a basic value of the family.

What to say?: "I get that you're mad, but we don't hit! You're showing me that you need to go play in a different room until you can remember to use your words and not your hands."

Kids don't ever misbehave for no reason. They are always trying to communicate something to us.

When our kids act out, we need to ask ourselves,

- What is my child unable to articulate with words?
- Is he scared/sad/mad/needing attention?
- What's making him feel this way?
- Is she feeling overwhelmed and doesn't know how to ask for help?
- Is something bothering her at school (or elsewhere) and she doesn't have the tools to deal with it – thereby, taking it out at home?
- Did he hear these words at school and is looking to us to see what to do with them?

When our kids are struggling, they need our help. When we lose our temper and punish them, they aren't any further along in figuring out what to do than they were before. We need to be investigators for our kids. Figuring out the underlying truth behind our kids' behavior. **Then, we need to teach them what we wish they would have said from the beginning.**

If my daughter is hungry, she doesn't realize that her blood sugar has taken a dive. Instead, she completely loses it over absolutely nothing. Her sister could simply look at her from across the room and she's down for the count. Crying, complaining, whining…it's all over! She's not yet tuned in with what her body needs, all she knows is that she can't cope with ANYTHING! She also knows that she can't bring herself back from the brink. She's just gone and anyone within a 5 mile radius lives in a loud and tortured place right along with her.

After we've gotten a side of beef into her and she's calmer, we talk about what just happened. If she could have simply told me that she was hungry, we could have gotten a handle on the situation before the nuclear meltdown in the middle of my kitchen. Our task is to make the connection for her. After 1,000 times of reflecting on why she's struggling, perhaps she'll be able to make the connection herself and say, "Mommy, I'm hungry!"

Love tanks

Another reason many kids have meltdowns is because their "LOVE

TANKS" are empty. I use the visual of a love tank because we all understand the concept of a tank being full and empty. When we give our kids lots of love and attention, we are filling up their love tanks. When we are too busy to pay much attention to them or haven't been around them at all, we are working on the reserves and eventually the tank becomes empty.

Some kids need more attention than other kids. For some, 24/7/365 attention would never be enough. For others, they are very self-sufficient and need only minimal time with us. It is our job as parents to give a reasonable amount of time and attention to let our kids know that they are important to us, but it is also our job to teach them that they are not the center of the universe. We need to prepare them for later on, when we're not around, when it finally dawns on them that they actually occupy only a small space in the world.

Kids don't always distinguish between positive and negative attention.

They are happy just to get any part of us. Unfortunately, we sometimes teach them to get our negative attention and so they are somewhat satisfied with that and willing to take whatever we will give them. I liken the different types of attention to the difference between eating a sugary snack and a high-protein snack.

When we eat a sugary snack, we are likely to crave more sugar in a very short time. When we eat a high-protein snack, we are satisfied for longer and can wait quite a while before eating again.

Attention is very similar. When we give our kids our negative attention (yelling, snapping, irritation, etc...) they are happy to have a piece of us, but they are likely to need more of our attention sooner. If we give them some undivided attention that includes cuddles, loves, approval, and other types of positive attention, we are likely to have filled up their tanks and find that they are quite satisfied for a longer period of time.

Ok, we all lose it sometimes. Even I do! Remember that newspaper headline? What parent doesn't get pushed to the brink and then doesn't want to pull back because the screaming feels so good and so deserved? The truth is, it's not productive and it certainly isn't good modeling. We need to hold it together so our kids learn healthy ways of handling their most challenging feelings.

Model
Good
Behavior

Many parents who come to see me in my office have needy kids who are driving them crazy. I often ask about the type of attention they are giving that child and how much time they spend giving them loving attention (reading books, laughing, tickling, hugging, etc...) For many families, my prescription of simply giving that child 10 minutes out of every hour with loving attention completely eliminates the needy, clingy and negative ways that the child asks for attention.

I also see many families in which the addiction to negative attention has taken on a life of its own. It becomes the default way that the members of the family relate to one another and then other issues get layered one by one on top until we have a mountain of bad behavior on the parts of both the kids and the parents and chaos ensues.

Peeling the layers back MUST START WITH THE PARENTS to make things better. When the parents begin to behave in more appropriate ways, then they can begin to teach their children. In the meltdown example, parents can begin to teach their kids what is really going on and how they wish their kids would handle it instead of the meltdown.

This is the *Parenting Backwards* part. Ask yourself how you would want your child to handle low blood sugar 30 years from now. Rather than my daughter screaming, carrying-on, rolling herself into a fetal position on the floor and crying like she's being brutally attacked, I would prefer that she ask herself what's going on and begin to try different measures starting with a healthy snack or a glass of orange juice. Thirty years from now, she might be working in a company or home raising her own children or both. There's no luxury of time to meltdown, nor is it productive or professional behavior.

Beginning today, I have to give her the tools to get through those moments.

- She needs to recognize that something's up.
- She needs to then identify what it is.
- She needs to problem-solve how she might remedy the situation appropriate for the situation.
- She needs to hold it together until a solution can be implemented.

These are the steps I need to walk her through today so that she will be able to walk herself through them as an adult.

Choosing your battles

When the pattern is arguing, struggling, negotiating for hours on end, day after day, parents need to first ask themselves:

WILL THIS MATTER 30 YEARS FROM NOW? (*Parenting Backwards!*)

If not, let go of it. Whenever there is a struggle, it is essential to pull out of that boxing ring. Avoid a struggle but keep the parental hierarchy firmly in place.

How to handle the situation?
How would you want the child to handle it in 30 years?
What can I teach him today that will begin to prepare him for 30 years from now?

One of the biggest hiccups that parents experience in setting limits with their kids is guilt.

There are so many reasons that parents feel guilty saying "no" or struggle to put limits in place and enforce them. Divorce is one reason. If parents are only with their kids for part of the week or have visitation weekends, they don't want to make their kids mad or spend their limited time together dealing with rules. They want it all to be happy. The truth is that kids need their parents to teach them boundaries and to let them know when they have stepped outside of the lines.

Other reasons that many parents avoid setting limits may include:
- They want their kids to like them
- They hated when their own parents were very strict and go too far the other way
- They're afraid of their child's anger or wrath

When we don't set appropriate limits, we communicate to our kids that their worth in the family is greater than it really is. I don't mean to say that our kids aren't worth their weight in gold – of course they are! However, teaching them humility is an essential part of what we must teach.

At 3 years old, kids learn that they have a great deal of control and influence over their environment – and they're not afraid to use it. We must make sure that we are still expecting them to be only three years old. When kids get a little full of themselves, their sense of self becomes inflated and they begin to take on a bigger persona than what is appropriate.

Three-year-olds need to be three; four-year-olds need to be four and so on. It is our job to ensure that they are only taking up that amount of space in the family and the world and no more!

The way that we show our kids their appropriate space is by letting them know through our limit-setting that WE KNOW BETTER FOR OUR KIDS THAN THEY KNOW FOR THEMSELVES. That is the secret to fearless limit-setting. That's why they have parents and that's our job, plain and simple.

When we are taking care of business, they are free to grow and explore and be a kid. They aren't bogged down with the weight of the world and decision-making and, therefore, the anxiety that goes along with those responsibilities. (I know I've said that before, but it bears repeating.)

Wouldn't you like someone to take unnecessary responsibilities away from you? Well, it may not happen for you, but do your kids a favor and do it for them!

Chapter Eight

Creating Your Parenting Tool Belt

"We shall neither fail nor falter; we shall not weaken or tire. Give us the tools and we will finish the job." Winston Churchill

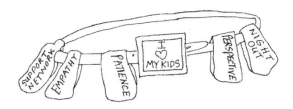

Like any good worker, parents need a well-stocked tool belt to ensure that they have the right tool for any given situation. Of course, even the handiest of handymen use the wrong screwdriver at times and need to find one that fits better in order to accomplish the task. The same is true for parents.

There are many different tools. Parents need to figure out what tools best fit their parenting needs. They might be different for everybody. Here is a list of some of my favorite tools that I find most useful in my parenting tool belt:

- Compassion
- Listening
- Humor
- Lead them by the shoulders
- "Uh Oh!"
- "Let me know…"
- E.Q.
- Selfish parenting
- Will this matter in 25 years?

Don't be afraid to try these tools – don't be afraid to make mistakes – don't be afraid to test their limits. The more you use your tools, the more familiar you become with their power and their limitations.

Compassion

The first tool I want to introduce to you is the tool of compassion. When our kids are acting up or simply just annoying us, having compassion stops your nerve-endings from wanting to lash out due to the intense frustration and discomfort. Having compassion enables you to take a step back, figure out WHY your child is behaving this way and then you can create an alliance rather than an adversarial relationship, trying to convince someone that he should change his behavior. That rarely works, by the way.

For example, when my daughter is especially clingy and needy, I sometimes just want to peel her off of me and tell her to get away. Sometimes, it just gets to be too much. In reality, getting mad at her and sending her away will only perpetuate the clingy and needy behavior. If I behave in a much more compassionate manner and give her the undivided attention she's craving, she's much more likely to get what she needs and go on her merry way. In addition, she feels like I totally get what she's going through and when she walks away she's happy knowing I'm there for her.

Listening

Many kids simply want to be heard, but in our haste of getting through our hectic daily schedules, we haven't allotted enough time to really listen to what our kids are trying to tell us. In addition, some preschoolers' stories can drone on and on while attempting to get to the point of the story. (Truth be told!)

I love to understand the inner workings of my kids' minds and I think it makes kids feel incredibly loved when they are truly listened to and understood to their core.

This is especially important when we have a child who completely boggles our minds (which most of them do). Maybe that child is more like your husband or wife and you just can't understand what makes either one of them tick. That's when the trick of listening and figuring them out is most important.

I also understand that listening to a toddler ramble on and on about a make-believe story or even the minute details of what happened at preschool can be difficult at times…even torturous! As parents, we have to strike a balance of listening with also honoring our kids by not pretending to care when we don't really care at all. By the way, they can tell when you're not listening!!!

If the story is going on and on, it's ok to ask them to finish the story or to "bottom line it" for you. This also teaches our kids not to become the adult at the party who rambles on and everyone can't wait to get away from them! You know that person? It's our job to let them know when enough is enough or even how to tell a long story in a short amount of time.

"Make 'em laugh, make 'em laugh, make 'em laugh..."

Parenting is pretty serious business. Honestly, the stakes are pretty high so doing a good job is important. Heck, it's important enough for me to write this book, right?

Rather than taking the job so seriously and making everyone crazy in the process, be sure to lighten things up at times. Don't take yourself so seriously, don't take your kids' misbehavior so personally and have fun once in a while.

The "tickle monster" has saved many intense moments in my house. So has laughing at myself. Sometimes, some self-deprecating humor is the best medicine.

Infusing some humor into your parenting will be one of the greatest things you do not only for your kids, but for yourself as well. A good, hearty belly-laugh has been likened to a full session of psychotherapy. It releases happy hormones into your body and just gives you a feeling of well-being.

One day, my daughter was being a bit ornery – ok, let's be honest, she was downright obnoxious. She had a chip on her shoulder and was ordering me around like the slave that I often am. I decided that rather than pouring more fuel onto her cranky fire, I would add some levity and attempt to make her laugh. At worst, I would get a chuckle out of it and at least one of us would feel better. I said to her, "Just for today, let's pretend that I'm the mom and YOU'RE the kid." As expected, she didn't think it was very funny, though it did catch her a bit off guard. As for me, I totally cracked myself up! Mission accomplished!

Lead them by the shoulders

How often do you feel like a complete nag? Daily? Hourly? Constantly? Me, too! I totally get it! My personal pet peeve is stuff being left around the house that I have to navigate around in an effort to preserve my sanity and my dignity – after all, falling is so embarrassing!

How many times do I have to remind them to put their stuff away? Clean up their toys, shoes, dirty socks, an endless supply of sweatshirts, plates, grape stems, cups, etc... (Shall I go on? Ugh!)

Somehow, however, I end up being the mean one in the equation – because I walk around the house and rarely have anything nice to say. I'm reminding and nagging and complaining that there is "stuff" EVERYWHERE!!!

I had to come up with another way to get things accomplished. So, here's my tool:

Ask them once and then give them a chance to do it. That's actually one of the mistakes I made, at first. I nagged again too soon. I didn't really give them a chance to do it. I wanted it done on my time schedule, not theirs. It wasn't very respectful. If I had a time concern,

I needed to express that upfront. If, in a reasonable amount of time it still wasn't done, I did the LEAD THEM BY THE SHOULDERS method. This means that without a word, I would gently place my hands behind their shoulders and lead them firmly and respectfully over to whatever I was hoping they would clean up. They got the message pretty quickly.

"Uh oh"

This is another tool that I really like. When I come upon the toys (or whatever) still strewn across my floor, I say to my child, "UH-OH!" I think this communicates with great respect that "I'm sure you just forgot to do this." Of course, I know better, but giving my child the benefit of the doubt is just a nice thing to do and encourages them to be respectful back when I'm not fighting to get her to do what I want her to do.

"Let me know…"

Another one of my favorites! "Let me know when you're ready to go!" This is a great way to withdraw from the power struggle of getting a three-year-old out of the house in the morning. It's also a great way to withdraw from the power struggle of what's appropriate to wear with a teenager.

This phrase communicates that you're not willing to engage in a battle, but that you'll patiently wait for your child to make the appropriate choice. Like "uh oh", it's very respectful and helps you, the parent, maintain your role as the authority.

E.Q.

Just like utilizing compassion rather than fighting against your child's behavior, it's much more productive to figure out why your child is behaving in this way and then educate him in the hopes that eventually he will use his words rather than his behavior to tell you that he's having a hard time.
We've spoken about Emotional Intelligence already, but I wanted to include it here as well. Labeling the feeling and having compassion for what our kids are feeling is a great tool to stop the battle, to avoid the meltdown and to simply help your child know what to do with the free-floating emotion running through his body. Feel free to take a look back at the EQ section in Chapter 5 to refresh your memory.

Selfish parenting

Parenting is a pretty selfless job, but many parents do **too much** for their kids. They are over-indulged and as a result they grow up to believe that the world was created only for them and that they are entitled to whatever they want whenever and however they want it. This can be quite frustrating for many parents. The first thing to be aware of is when you feel that frustration, some boundary has been violated. Where does a limit need to be set?

I encourage parents to be a little bit selfish in their parenting. Now, if you tend to spend 6 hours a day getting massages and basically finding every excuse not to be with your kids, this section is NOT for you. I'm talking to you parents who tend to do too much for your kids and spend every waking minute attending to their every whim.

Be a little more selfish. Put your own needs ahead of your kids'. It good for them to learn that adults come first and that their own needs are not the most important things in the world.

We also need to teach our kids delayed gratification. Learning to wait is a very good thing and strengthens a muscle that will come in very handy in adulthood. There have been studies that show that delayed gratification has a high correlation with success later in life. Think about it, if your kids are able to delay their desire to go do something they WANT to do in favor of something they NEED to do, wouldn't that make sense that they are more likely to be successful? For example, in college if our kids are able to delay partying in favor of studying, they are certainly more likely to be successful in passing their classes. It also gives them a better sense of priorities and stronger self-esteem because they can then be proud of themselves for their accomplishments. There's no limit to the benefits of delayed gratification!

In addition, a little selfish parenting will also teach kids to have respect for your authority as parents. By taking care of yourself, you are communicating to your kids that YOU are important, too. This will help you to maintain that sense of power that you need in order for your kids to respect your limits and your words, in general. That is certainly lacking in our society these days. At the risk of sounding like an old curmudgeon, kids these days just don't have enough respect for authority. We need to maintain our hierarchy in our homes so that when our kids are in school they will be respectful to their teachers and administrators as well as be respectful of their bosses as they enter the work world. Without that respect, they are setting themselves up for many failures and an inability to function in a society where hierarchies exist in most work settings.

Choosing your Battles

WILL THIS MATTER IN 25 or 30 YEARS?

I know I have already mentioned this, but it's one of the cornerstones of the *Parenting Backwards* philosophy and is an essential tool in the *Parenting Backwards* Tool Belt!

The battles you choose to take on should not be just a matter of how much energy you have in the moment, as is the case for many parents. I want you to be much more intentional than that.

When deciding whether or not to take on your kid on a given issue, ask yourself if this issue translated into the future would it matter 25 years from now. For example, if your child is being disrespectful to you in how he's speaking, ask yourself, "would it be ok if he did this to his boss 25 years from now?" I'm thinking the answer is an emphatic "YES!" It would definitely matter, so that's a battle you need to address whether you have the energy for it or not. (This doesn't mean that you should engage in a power struggle, it means that it's time to set a limit!)

If your child leaves his toys all over the floor of his room, it might be quite annoying while trying to sneak in and play tooth fairy, but let's think ahead 25 years. If your son, as a grown man, left his clothes all over the floor of his house could he still have a responsible and productive life? Absolutely! Of course, his spouse might be incredibly annoyed with him, but it might not be a deal-breaker. Just close the door to his room and use a flashlight when being the tooth fairy! (This is only after teaching your values of keeping your space clean and the benefits of having a clean room – for those of you who are ready to scream at me.)

Chapter 9

Have Faith!

Teaching the Values of Faith, Hope, Optimism and the Importance of Community

"Faith is a knowledge within the heart, beyond the reach of proof." Kahlil Gibran

You're probably wondering why I would include this topic in a parenting book. It doesn't tell you how to get your kids to behave better…or does it? What faith, hope and optimism do for our kids is give them a sense of purpose in their lives as well as the coping skills to believe that the difficult times will get better.

Life is a complex mixture of ups and downs. Sometimes we know when the good times are coming and sometimes they come as a welcome and unexpected pleasure. It isn't, however, my intention to focus on the good times because I don't think it takes much effort to prepare our kids for the good things that life has to offer. My intention in writing this book is to give parents the tools to prepare their kids for the rough times. Those aren't so easy. Rough times come in many different packages. The important thing is to stop, be in your child's shoes in that moment and draw upon the compassion that we've spoken about. It is important to maintain perspective so that you give the proper amount of emotional energy to help them get them through it, to learn from it and, more important, to move forward. There is also a time when we need to stay back and let them try their wings. If they fall, we'll be there, but if we step in too early, we might be robbing them of the opportunity to try out their own skills and thereby feel good about themselves and their own abilities.

I can draw upon two different experiences of my own. My daughter Lauren didn't make the dance team when she tried out for it. In that moment, her world fell apart. My job was to be sad with her, but to also help her understand that this was an opportunity for her to find something else to be passionate about. In the end, she did find the Color guard team and that experience not only gave her friendships, but also her most fond memories of high school.

Also, going back to my story of our beloved dog, Havi. In my children's world at that time, this was the first deep loss that they had ever experienced of a loved one. It was important for us to walk them through the stages of grief, to move forward while always keeping Havi in their hearts and being able to welcome and love the newest member of our family, Lacey. I truly believe that the loss of Havi also began to prepare them for the other inevitable losses to come in their lives.

Faith, hope and optimism are important coping skills to teach our kids. Faith can be a belief in anything. There is no one religion that is better than another, nor is it necessary to subscribe to a particular organized religion at all. Spiritual beliefs can come in many forms. I believe that it's the belief in something bigger than we are that is the essential element in addition to some meaningful rituals. This is the winning combination that enables us to have an anchor and a fall-back when times get hard and we aren't sure what to do with ourselves. (By the way, I do believe that Atheists can also raise great kids with healthy coping skills!)

Rituals create a direction for our actions, and faith in something bigger than we are. They also give us the hope that perhaps the situation is more than we can see and comprehend from our limited perspective. This opens up the possibility for hope that things will get better – even the things beyond our own control.

Religious or spiritual rituals truly are the anchor in the storm during rough times. Jewish rituals around death and mourning are a good example. They are designed to honor the grieving. The pain is cushioned with family, friends and community surrounding the griever for the first 7 days almost around the clock. By the end of that week, the bereaved will probably be happy to have everyone go home.

The rituals that go from there look at the 30 day mark and then the one year mark, all the while surrounding the loved ones with community – never allowing them to say their traditional prayers alone. How amazing is that?

People I have known who have truly followed the Jewish traditions through the traditional one year process have said that at the end of that period of time, they truly felt done with their grief process. That doesn't mean that they stop missing their loved one, but they do feel ready to move on with their lives. The religion creates the roadmap that is for many people uncharted territory.

Hope

Hope is the single most important ingredient in reducing depression, suicidality, and even anxiety. Where there is hope, there is a belief in the future and an open door to optimism. Model hope for your kids and teach them that there is never a hopeless situation, only opportunities for something perhaps unexpected.

Community

Sharing a sense of community is a big part of teaching our kids hope. A community creates a sense of belonging and provides a context in which our kids understand themselves, who they are, what they believe and even what to do with themselves during tough times.

A community helps us define ourselves and provides support through the rough spots of life. Friendships, extended family relationships, churches and synagogues, clubs, groups, etc…are all ways that we define ourselves and learn how to be ourselves in a social context.

I learned how to be a mom from my fellow moms – watching them, listening to how they talked to their kids, even deciding what I didn't like and chose not to emulate. For many years, my girlfriends have been my extended family. My husband doesn't want to hear my every thought, but my girlfriends do!

Going for long walks with my girlfriends is almost as good as therapy! We'll go for miles and not even realize how far we've walked. We talk about everything – really share and connect – and solve the ills of the world. It's very cathartic!

These are my Bunco Babes!!

One of my greatest joys is playing Bunco with my Bunco Babes. Though, we have scattered in recent months, the camaraderie and support that group provided was beyond valuable. We kept each other apprised of what was going on in our kids' schools, with our kids' friends, and with each other. We supported each other through deaths, divorces, struggles and joys. I remember one of our pacts. When our kids were all getting their drivers' licenses, we were all scared to death. It was understood that, as moms, we would all watch the road for each others' kids. Our kids knew that whenever they were driving, many eyes were on them. They'd better come to a complete stop and they'd better drive the speed limit and, God forbid, they'd better not text while driving! (Thank you, Ladies!)

A sense of community and belonging eliminates feelings of isolation which is part of hopelessness and depression. Have you ever heard that misery loves company? It's so true!!

Being a part of a community also helps people feel a sense of responsibility to give back to that community. When someone you know is sick, it's natural to want to step in and bring soup or shuttle kids for her. That's the beauty of creating an extended family. The give and take of that community gives your children a feeling of belonging and purpose. Remember, they're watching and listening!

I, for one, really struggle with accepting help. I was raised to be fiercely independent and feel as though it's a sign of weakness to allow someone to do my job. I have learned, however, not only the joy of giving to others, but also the joy in allowing others to help me. I'm learning to simply say, "thank you" and stop there. An exercise that you might try, too!

There is another level of giving back that a community demands and that your children need to learn. That is providing the basic needs of needy families in your community. For families that are able, it is essential to donate canned goods to your local food bank, bring dinners to your local church or synagogue that provides meals for the homeless, donating old clothing, shoes, coats and blankets to provide for the neediest in your community. These are very concrete ways to teach our kids gratitude and the importance of thinking of others.

There are also charities all around that provide services that are always in need of something. As parents, we need to teach our kids to feel a sense of responsibility to and compassion for them. From donating last year's coat that's too small, to actually going and serving food. This is the responsibility of each of us and helps us to teach our kids to remember what is truly important and to be grateful for their blessings.

When we do for others, we are – even temporarily – outside of ourselves. This is a great lesson in giving back, in humility, but it is also an unexpected antidote to depression. When we are focused on our own pain, it's hard to know that feeling good is an option. When we are doing for others, we can't help but feel good on the inside and even forget our own troubles for a time.

Optimism

Optimism is a way of thinking, a belief system and a philosophy...maybe even a way of life. It's defined as:

op·ti·mism –noun
1. a disposition or tendency to look on the more favorable side of events or conditions and to expect the most favorable outcome.
2. the belief that good ultimately predominates over evil in the world.
3. the belief that goodness pervades reality.
4. the doctrine that the existing world is the best of all possible worlds.

I think a lot of the sections of this book are important and should be separate books unto themselves. Optimism, is probably my favorite and the most important section of this book. Why? Because optimism is the antidote to all of the misery in our lives. Of course, simply being optimistic doesn't solve all our problems. We have to be proactive, resourceful and perseverant. However, along the road of this life, having a positive attitude sure makes the journey more enjoyable. It also makes you more enjoyable to be around.

We cannot promise our kids a life of ease and trouble-free living. However, **by teaching our kids to see the world through an optimistic lens, we give them the gift of hope when the going gets tough, we give them the gift of belief that things will get better, we give them the ability to rise above the negative feelings of the situation and to see the blessings even in troubling times.**

Chapter 10

Letting go!
The Value of Independence and Self-Reliance

"Some of us think holding on makes us strong, but sometimes it is letting go." — Herman Hesse

Every stage of raising our kids involves a new level of letting go. Birth is the first separation when our kids literally separate from our bodies and begin to breathe on their own. From there, it just continues. Next comes weaning. When our kids no longer depend upon our bodies for their nourishment, many moms experience profound sadness. All right, it's also a hormone withdrawal, but losing that closeness with your child is sad for many moms.

After weaning, come crawling and walking. Once our kids can walk away from us, they are less likely to want us to hold them and they begin to wander farther and farther away. Their exploration of the world has begun and their need of us begins to wane.

Then, they begin preschool. Up until now, we know all of their friends; we know everything they know because (if we're lucky enough to have been home with them) we were there when they learned it. When they start preschool or day care, suddenly, they develop relationships of which we are not a part, they are learning things that we aren't present for and they begin to find their own personalities and styles of relating in groups.

The separations continue through kindergarten, grade school, middle school and the obvious separation that is adolescence.

It's kind of cruel. We give birth and fall completely in love with and attached to these little people. They need us for their very survival and we need to be needed by them.

Then, the rules change on us. It becomes our job to make our kids independent. They need to learn to walk the world on their own and they need to learn to draw upon the strength that we have given them and to know that we will always be there if they fall.

This is where a lot of parents go awry. In my private practice, I see some parents who have not let their little ones develop an age-appropriate sense of independence. Kids need to be able to make some decisions for themselves (which short-sleeved shirt, for example, for preschoolers) while parents balance not giving them too much responsibility with giving them appropriate choices and consequences.

In addition to responsibilities, kids need to develop a sense of self-reliance. As I mentioned before, the first opportunity parents have to teach their kids self-reliance is with sleep training. This is the first time the parents assert themselves as "the parents" and say "I know better for you than you know for yourself." They have to switch the rules of comfort and allow kids to tolerate discomfort rather than fixing it for them.

This is where it all begins. Teaching kids to tolerate discomfort at an early age makes it easier to teach them to tolerate discomfort all along the way as they grow. (I know we've talked about this before! It's THAT important!)

How do we do this?

- We let them tough the little things out on their own – when it doesn't seem cruel.

- We allow them to wait and delay their gratification whenever possible.
- We don't make everything all better for them.
- We have compassion for them, but ask them to push through.
- We expect them to recover in an appropriate amount of time rather than indulging their discomfort for an extended period.
- We allow our kids to feel the sting of the consequences of their poor choices and not fix everything for them.

Understand that all of our kids are different. I have three daughters who all handle situations differently. My oldest, who is my most sensitive, for example, cried every time I left the house for years. Of course, I cried, too, feeling as though I was torturing my child – even if I was just going to the market. Then, I figured her out. After I left a crying, hysterical child, I would call a short time later just to make sure she was ok. Of course, she was ok! I really needed that time away. It was how I recharged myself and came back a happier mommy.

I realized that the tears were, for the most part, for my benefit. She was testing to see how much power she had and if her tears were effective enough to get me to change my plans. Thankfully, I still went and taught her that I always came back. I would sing Hap Palmer's "My Mommy Comes Back" to her as I left and when I arrived back home. Eventually, she found the song to be comforting. Having a transitional object, was also very helpful in her ability to comfort herself and handle the transitions as I would leave and come back. My three daughters had different objects. For one, it was a terry-cloth bear, for the other two, it was a small comfort silkie blanket. It doesn't matter what the object is, as long as it is comforting to them.

Separation anxiety is troubling for everyone involved, but your consistency and confidence that all will be well teaches the child to tolerate the discomfort of the separation and eventually shows the child that no matter how they behave when we leave, we are still leaving. So, they might as well be fine with it. Once their behavior effects us – we are theirs and all power is lost!

What about as they get older? Separation anxiety is nothing compared to watching your 16 year old drive away for the first time alone! How about the parents who continue to proofread or even to write their adult child's papers in college?

Our job is to begin the separation process a little bit at a time so that eventually, when the time comes for them to be on their own, they have all of the tools that they need to be successful without our day to day interference, and we have all of the career, hobbies, friends and volunteer opportunities that WE need to stay busy, too.

Chapter 11

Finding Your Passion and Remembering to Laugh

"Through humor, you can soften some of the worst blows that life delivers. And once you find laughter, no matter how painful your situation might be, you can survive it." Bill Cosby

Thank you all for walking this journey with me. Writing my first parenting book has been a labor of love for me and a passion of mine for many years. In my practice, I have helped many parents and children get through the best and worst of times. I have always felt that these experiences were worth putting down on paper in the hopes that they would help someone else.

In this final chapter, I'd like to talk about two important things to me in parenting. Finding your passion and remembering to laugh. In this chapter, I'd like to remind you that being a parent doesn't mean that you need to lose your identity. Parenting is one of the most wonderful, valuable and rewarding jobs that you will ever have. However, you are more than just a parent. You are a complex individual with talents, passions and the need to fulfill a sense of purpose beyond being a parent.

All of these parenting instructions, rules, do's and don'ts may seem overwhelming. In truth, we do so much without having to even think about it. Being intentional shouldn't be a burden, but really a gift of figuring out more easily how to handle any given situation, especially the tough ones.

When we have a basic philosophy to pull from, we aren't parenting from the hip, nor do we often feel at a loss to know what to do while raising our kids. We have a framework from which to draw when we really want to scream, spank, or have a tantrum ourselves.

It can all seem so serious, at times. We have to remember to laugh with our kids. My favorite times with my kids are around the dinner table or even in the car when something strikes us as funny and we are laughing until we cry.

There IS such a thing as over-parenting and even over-thinking. If you want to keep it really simple just keep in mind three things:

1. Who you want your kids to become 25-30 years from now?

2. What kind of relationship do you want to have with your kids – now and 30 years from now?

3. What culture do you want to have in your home? One of chaos or one of respect? Act accordingly and teach those values!

One great tip for avoiding the over-parenting trap or even to avoid over-indulging your kids, is to get or stay active in your own passions. If you love art, take art classes or at least paint at some point each week. If you love the theater, make sure you make theater a part of your life. If your secret fantasy is to be a singer, take voice lessons or just put on your favorite cd's and sing your heart out on a regular basis. Maybe you've dreamt of being an NBA star. Find a basketball team or get a group of friends together and play once a week. Whatever floats your boat, pay attention to that which makes your spirit soar. Nurture your interests and fill up your own buckets with things that make your soul sing. You'll be a happier parent, you'll feel more balanced as an individual, you'll be a joy to be around and you'll also show your children the beauty of finding their passions!

I hope that you have found a pearl or two in this book that you can take with you into your parenting – for you and /or for your kids.

Thank you for traveling this journey with me.

.

Who do you want your kids to be 25 – 30 years from now?

- Respectful?
- Responsible?
- Self-Reliant?
- Compassionate?
- A good friend?

What do you need to do today to achieve these goals?

Parenting Backwards is a philosophy with concrete how-to's for parents of kids of all ages!

Parenting Backwards is the owners' manual for raising kids to become fabulous adults.

About the Author

Bette Levy Alkazian is a Licensed Marriage and Family Therapist in Thousand Oaks, California. She has worked with parents of kids of all ages through her practice, *Balanced Parenting*, for many years.

In addition to her private therapy and parent coaching practice, Bette also does speaking engagements, parenting classes and writes in her spare time.

Bette has been married to her husband, Jeff, for 29 years and they have three, fabulous daughters.

Made in the USA
Middletown, DE
26 November 2017